the SECRET LANGUAGE of Dogs

Books of Merit

the SECRET LANGUAGE of Dogs

THE BODY LANGUAGE OF FURRY BODIES

Heather Dunphy

THOMAS ALLEN PUBLISHERS

TORONTO

Published by Thomas Allen Publishers,
a division of Thomas Allen & Son Limited,
390 Steelcase Road East
Markham, Ontario, L3R 1G2 CANADA

www.thomasallen.ca

Conceived, designed, and produced by:
Quid Publishing
Level 4 Sheridan House
114 Western Road
Hove BN3 1DD
England
www.quidpublishing.com

Design: Ali Walper
Cover image: © Glenn Nagel | Dreamstime

The publisher gratefully acknowledges the support
of The Ontario Arts Council for its publishing program.

We acknowledge the support of the Canada Council for the Arts, which
last year invested $20.1 million in writing and publishing throughout Canada.

We acknowledge the Government of Ontario through the
Ontario Media Development Corporation's Ontario Book Initiative.

We acknowledge the financial support of the Government of Canada through
the Canada Book Fund (CBF) for our publishing activities.

10 9 8 7 6 5 4 3 2 1

Printed and bound in Singapore

CONTENTS

Introduction 8

FIRST IMPRESSIONS
How Breed Characteristics Provide Insight 16

WELCOME HOME
Understand Each Other from Day One 26

DOG SENSE
Canine Interaction with Their Environment 34

CANINE COMMUNICATION
How Body Language Conveys Messages 46

GROWLING AS COMMUNICATION
The Meaning Behind the Message 58

WHINING AS COMMUNICATION
Are You There? 64

BARKING AS COMMUNICATION
It's More Than Just Noise 68

HOWLING AS COMMUNICATION
The Canine Calling Card 74

9

PACK DYNAMICS

In the Wild and in Your Home 78

10

CANINE TO CANINE

Interaction with Other Dogs 84

11

BEHAVIOR PROBLEM: AGGRESSION

Understand the Message 88

12

BEHAVIOR PROBLEM: CHEWING

How to Translate a Gnawing Problem 96

13

BEHAVIOR PROBLEM: DIGGING

A Guide to Understanding Why Dogs Dig 102

14

BEHAVIOR PROBLEMS: INAPPROPRIATE

Learned Behaviors We Teach Our Dogs 110

15

CANINE FAQS

A Guide to Understanding Common Questions 114

16

HEALTH 101

What Behavior and Appearance Changes Can Tell You 124

17

HOME HEALTH CHECK

Prevention Is Better than Treatment 128

18 SPEAK VOLUMES

How Dogs Interpret Our Actions 132

19 LOST IN TRANSLATION

How Dogs Interpret Our Mixed Messages 138

20 THE LEARNING CURVE

Intuitive and Teachable Learning 144

21 SIT, STAY, DOWN, COME

Speak the Language of Training 150

22 FUN AND GAMES

Mental and Physical Stimulation Through Play 160

23 AGES AND STAGES

Puppyhood and Adolescence 170

24 AGES AND STAGES

The Older Dog 176

Glossary 180

Acknowledgments 182

Picture Credits 183

Bibliography 186

Index 188

INTRODUCTION

*O*nce upon a time, the languages of canines and humans were not so
disparate. Our cave-dwelling ancestors grunted their wishes to each other
and relied on body language to communicate, just as our dogs do. As words
were formed, our languages, although always different, moved further apart.
Human language evolved and became primarily vocal, relying less and less on body
language. We still use it, of course, but as a secondary tool in communication,
meant to emphasize our verbal vocabulary. This hampers our ability to
communicate with our dogs, who are experts at sending and receiving messages
through body language. They use vocalization as well—and very impressively,
as the different intensities and tones of the growl, whine, bark, and howl all
attest—but theirs is a different language, one that we can sometimes "speak" and
translate accurately, but very often get wrong. To speak your dog's language, you
must understand how your messages may be interpreted, what your dog's actions
signify, and how pack dynamics contribute to explanations of your dog's behavior.

GETTING THE MESSAGE

It is easy to forget that we can't interpret dog behavior as we would a human's behavior. Although we all communicate through facial expressions, body posture, movement, and vocalization our actions mean different things depending on the language used. For example, proof of a dog's guilt is often interpreted by how he averts his eyes or slinks away from us when we come home to find the couch cushions torn to pieces. But as far as the dog is concerned, chewing is a natural canine behavior. He doesn't know he did anything wrong, so he is not acknowledging guilt with his body language. Humans hang their heads in shame and look away when they are embarrassed. Our dogs don't. They simply look guilty to us because we have misunderstood their language, which

is not communicating guilt in this instance, but submission—a reaction to their owner's angry or frustrated tone and body language. The dog's "guilty look" has nothing to do with the chewed cushions. We only think it does when we interpret his body language as we would a human's, forgetting that canines communicate differently. Another example would be the dog who urinates in the house, waiting to do so until you walk in the door after an absence. This is often interpreted as deliberate behavior, but dogs are not being spiteful when they do this, and they don't urinate when they see us to act out their displeasure at being left alone. Our dogs don't think like that. In the canine world, rolling onto their back and urinating shows deference and is part of the pack behavior vocabulary learned as a pup. The dog is simply showing submissive behavior,

recognizing you as a more dominant member of his canine-people pack. Without an understanding of canine vocabulary we don't always understand what is being communicated, and too often interpret canine messages according to our—very different— language. We attribute human responses and motivation to our dogs and these anthropomorphic tendencies—that a dog acts as we do—contributes to misunderstandings that could be avoided if we remember that dogs are dogs, not four-legged humans who feel and react to things as we do.

 Dog Fact

The actions and appearance of your dog are the only way he can communicate what he is feeling. Key to reading the signs is understanding what is normal for your dog, and when change signifies a message.

SENDING A MESSAGE

You can talk to your dog for hours and even though he won't understand a word he will still receive and interpret messages from you. Much is communicated through our body language and tone of voice, but because we speak such very different languages it is easy to send messages we didn't intend. To us, making direct eye contact is a friendly gesture. Not so with our dogs, who use direct eye contact to communicate a threat. Tone of voice is also important to consider. If we respond to an aggressive dog with an angry voice it may be clear to other people that we don't like the aggressive behavior, but to our dogs it sends a different message. Aggressiveness is often a result of fear;

an angry tone of voice tells the dog he was right to feel threatened and enhances his fear, and thus increases the intensity of his behavior. In the same way, when we use a high-pitched tone to comfort and soothe a dog who is cowering in fright from a thunderstorm we are reinforcing his fear. A calm and matter-of-fact tone communicates that everything is okay, but when we see our dogs frightened our first impulse is not to sound like it is business as usual. We instead talk to our dogs in an uncharacteristic voice meant to sound happy and soothing. As we become fluent in canine communication we learn that the message we send by doing so is not what was intended. Our tone of voice in both instances— whether reacting to aggression or comforting our

HEALTHY COMMUNICATION

Our dogs communicate not only through their body language and vocalization, but also through their health. A dull coat may be a sign that your dog's diet is not providing the nutrition he needs. If your dog has developed a new mannerism, such as shaking his head vigorously and frequently, he may have ear mites. If your older dog is suddenly acting more aggressively he may be compensating with barks and growls for decreased vision or hearing, and the vulnerability that goes along with that. A loss or gain in weight may be a sign of health problems. Watch for the signs, not only from your dog's body language but also what his appearance communicates. Dogs are generally good at disguising signs of illness or pain; knowing what to look for is part of the secret language of dogs. Canny and attentive owners can decipher the signs to keep their dogs safe and healthy.

A Dog Is a Dog Is a Dog

There is an old saying, "A dog is a dog is a dog," which means that dogs, regardless of breed, behave in largely the same way. Although each dog has its own personality, all dogs share certain traits and behaviors. An understanding of their motivations, characteristics, and behavior leads to many eureka moments, when suddenly the reasons for a certain behavior become evident. When this happens, our communication, and therefore the bond we enjoy with our dogs, is enhanced.

dog in a thunderstorm—tells him we are not in control. In the wild, the alpha dog doesn't have to communicate loudly to get his point across and a higher pitch is interpreted as fearful or childish—not the voice of a leader who can be trusted. Humans are primates and dogs are canids—two very different species with different social cues and body language. Our dogs get to know us, and we them, through the messages we send. It is important we don't send out the wrong message unintentionally or misread their messages. A good relationship is based on good communication. Dogs communicate differently, but it is something that can be learned, resulting in better-behaved and happier dogs, and an enhanced people–canine bond. Learning any new language takes practice, but fluency in the canine language is repaid tenfold. Owning a dog is proven to enhance quality of life. Investing the time to understand each other can only be beneficial to you and your dog.

FIRST IMPRESSIONS

HOW BREED CHARACTERISTICS PROVIDE INSIGHT

W̸hich breed is right for you? Sharing your life with a dog is a long-term decision, so careful consideration is needed before welcoming one into your home and life. There are more than 150 recognized breeds, each split into a group that shares traits for which the dogs were bred.

Dogs of the "herding group" were initially bred to control the movements of other animals, and this trait is still evident in the Collie, Australian Cattle Dog, and Pembroke Welsh Corgi, for example, when they affectionately try to herd their family. Breeds of the "sporting group" were bred to be active, so potential owners know that if they add a Cocker Spaniel, Irish Setter, or Pointer to their families these dogs are going to require much physical activity. Dogs of the "working group" needed to be strong and dedicated, as they were originally bred to perform rescues, and as sled or guard dogs. Of course, these dogs would be powerfully built, as seen in the German Shepherd—popular with families as well as being a leading breed with the police and military.

Breed characteristics can communicate much about a dog's temperament, activity levels, and needs, all of which can help you decide if your lifestyle is suited to the breed. If you want a long-distance running mate, look at breeds with high activity levels, or, if your idea of a perfect canine companion is a

dog that sheds minimally, then one of the single-coated breeds may be your best match. Given the number of breeds, it is impossible to list the details of each here, but the following practicalities will help you define your criteria, and start you on your way to understanding the language of breeds, and which one is right for you.

 Dog Fact

Understanding breed characteristics can be instructive, but remember that temperament and personality are individual to each dog.

COAT CARE

All dogs need regular coat care, but the amount of time needed differs according to breed. The elegant long coat of the Afghan Hound is beautiful, but it is important to see past the appearance and recognize the significant grooming needed to maintain it. Do you have the time and inclination to commit to this? Grooming is not simply for aesthetic reasons; it is necessary in order to keep the coat and skin healthy. Tangled and matted hair pulls at a dog's skin and can lead to irritation, hot spots, and fungus or insect infestation. Twice-weekly brushing may be enough for some breeds, while others will also need regular haircuts. Many breeds, like the Pekingese and Briard, need daily coat care. Certain shorthaired breeds, like Pugs, Boxers, or Whippets, require minimal brushing (but may need other grooming, such as bi-weekly skin care in the case of Pugs).

SHEDDING

Most dogs shed hair, but the amount they shed, and the timing, varies by breed. Some breeds shed year-round, some shed seasonally in spring or fall, or when losing their puppy coat for their adult coat. High-shedding dogs like the Dalmatian shed year-round. Double-coated breeds, such as the Akita, Shetland Sheepdog, and Samoyed, are wonderful companions but may also shed heavily, so you will need to accept the dog hair that comes with them. Although regular grooming can help control shedding, the amount a dog sheds does not dictate their grooming needs. The curly and sometimes corded single coat of the Poodle requires a great deal of grooming but sheds minimally; the short, silky hair of the single-coated Italian Greyhound needs only an occasional brushing and a rub-down with a towel and sheds little. How much dog hair—on your furniture, in your car, and on your clothes—can you live with?

NOTHING TO SNEEZE AT

It is not dog hair that causes pet allergies, it is the dander—extremely small skin flakes that become airborne. No breed is 100 percent hypoallergenic as they all produce dander, even hairless breeds. Low-shedding coats, however, typically produce less than others and may be a breath of fresh air for allergy sufferers, reducing the risk of itchy eyes, a runny nose, sneezing, or sinus problems. Breeds to consider include, but are not limited to: Bedlington Terrier, Bichon Frise, Cairn Terrier, Chinese Crested, Coton de Tulear, Havanese, Irish Water Spaniel, Kerry Blue Terrier, Maltese, Poodle, Portuguese Water Dog, Schnauzer, Shih Tzu, Soft Coated Wheaten Terrier, Yorkshire Terrier, and Xoloitzcuintli. Spend time with the breed you are considering prior to bringing one home in order to ascertain how they might affect those with allergies.

ENERGY LEVEL

Breed is indicative of energy level, but it really depends on the individual dog. Some dogs love nothing more than a long run and are built for endurance, while others prefer to curl up on the couch with you. High-energy breeds like the Pyrenean Shepherd, Brittany, or German Pointer don't just enjoy physical exercise, they need it, and can become destructive if deprived. Of course, all dogs need a daily walk and run, but most of the toy breeds—like Pomeranians and Yorkshire Terriers—happily fulfill their exercise needs with a short walk and indoor play. Consider how energetic you are and how much time per day you can devote to exercise with your dog.

SOCIABILITY

Dogs that are exposed from a young age to children, pets, and strangers are more comfortable with them because they have been socialized properly, but a breed's temperament should be also be considered. Boston Terriers and Labrador Retrievers typically love the company of other dogs and children in the home, while Chihuahuas may not be recommended for homes with small children but generally get along with other pets. Bulldogs usually coexist well with children and cats, are sociable with strangers, but don't always get along with other dogs. Boxers can be guarded with strangers, but playful with their human family. Will your dog live with children or other pets, and will there be frequent visitors to your home?

Shedding Some Light

Dog shedding is a natural process that varies by age and breed. Many puppies shed when they lose their puppy coat for their adult coat. Some breeds with double coats—a soft undercoat and coarser outer coat—may shed heavily twice a year, in a process known as "blowing" a coat. These breeds shed their undercoat seasonally in spring or fall to allow for a new coat; in the fall the hair is shed to make way for a heavier coat that will keep them warm in the colder months, and in the spring this process may be reversed.

SIZE

Puppies grow quickly, and some—like the large breeds such as the Mastiff and Great Dane—grow to a large size. It's important to think about the adult size of the breed and how that will fit with your lifestyle.

SPACE

As long as daily exercise needs are met, big dogs don't always need big homes, but the amount of space you have will be perfect for some breeds and unsuitable for others. The docile Italian Greyhound is a large breed that is very relaxed indoors and can live quite happily in a small home. The Great Pyrenees is a large breed that needs lots of space; despite their modest exercise requirements they are very independent and like to roam, and need space to run and play. The Old English Sheepdog is an example of a breed that lives well in a small or large home. They are well-mannered dogs that are sometimes described as couch potatoes—of course this is only after working off their energy outdoors. Dogs from the "toy group," like the Papillion or Yorkshire Terrier, are little dogs with big personalities who do well in apartments, as do many small breeds outside of the toy group, like the Schipperke.

Dog Fact

The terms "mixed breed" and "crossbreed" are often used interchangeably, but their meanings are different. Both are dogs whose parents are from different breeds, but crossbreed refers to the intentional crossing of two different purebred dog breeds. Rarely does the breeding of mixed-breed dogs happen intentionally.

MIXED BREEDS: A LITTLE OF THIS, A LITTLE OF THAT

Mixed-breed dogs share two very important qualities with purebred dogs: each canine—regardless of ancestry—is unique, and all are capable of making wonderful family members. With the purebred dog, the characteristics of their breed provide insight into which traits that dog is likely to carry. The genetics, however, are a useful guide, not a guarantee. A mixed-breed dog has parents from two different purebred or mixed-breed dogs, and this means he shares characteristics from both. He may look recognizably like a Beagle or a Collie, for example. Or, it may be difficult to discern what genetic code he inherited. It is likely that you won't know much about the parents or which of their characteristics—adult size, temperament, needs—the mixed-breed dog will favor. He could be gentle or aggressive, mischievous, obedient, or stubborn, gregarious, healthy, or sickly, and any combination of these—but because environment plays a major role in a dog's future behavior the same could be said of the purebred dog. If the dog's needs are met in a loving environment he will return the favor tenfold, whether purebred or mixed breed. In the end, it comes down to the care, socialization, and training a dog gets. These define the individual dog, and the joy of pet ownership can be experienced regardless of pedigree.

BEHIND THE SIGNS

Dog Fact

Many breeds retain the strong drives and instincts—hunting or herding, for example—for which they were bred.

How Many Dog Breeds Are There?

Canine registries throughout the world differ in the number of breeds they recognize and their categorization. Currently the American Kennel Club recognizes over 150 breeds, the New Zealand Kennel Club recognizes over 180 breeds, and the Kennel Club (UK) recognizes over 200 breeds. Category names may vary between country but can include the following groups: sporting, hound, working, terrier, gundog, pastoral, herding, utility, non-sporting, miscellaneous, and toy.

COMPANIONSHIP

All dogs need time and attention as well as physical and mental stimulation, but some breeds, like the Weimaraner, which loves attention and human companionship, may suffer more than others when left alone. If you work long hours or do not spend much time at home you may want to reconsider getting a dog of any breed. It is simply not fair to leave them alone for long periods of time.

WELCOME HOME

UNDERSTAND EACH OTHER FROM DAY ONE

First impressions are important. Whether you are bringing a puppy or adult dog into your home, the first week sets the tone of your relationship and forms the basis of understanding. A dog that is comfortable in his environment is ready to move from simply reacting to his new situation to interacting with what surrounds him—and that includes you.

Morning is the best time to welcome your dog home. It gives him the day to explore and settle in, as well as sufficient exercise and playtime to tire him out for his first night under your roof. The transition can be unsettling for a puppy who has never been apart from his mother and littermates, just as it can be for an adult dog who finds himself in unfamiliar surroundings. Everything is new and that brings uncertainty. Your goal is to communicate to your dog from the start that he is in a safe and loving environment. By introducing him to the house rules at an early stage he will feel at home more quickly because he knows what to expect, and what is expected of him. Start giving commands from the start, such as "sit" or "stay," and reward good behavior. A pup who hasn't had training yet may not understand, but an older dog will often already know the basic commands. Ignore any bad behavior. A stern "no" should be given, but anything more is just providing attention, and what you don't want to be communicating is that misbehavior is rewarded with attention. Ignoring the dog is enough of a punishment; anything more creates fear and confusion, and is not a foundation for good communication.

Dog Fact

Choose a name for a new puppy as soon as possible. Be consistent and use it repeatedly as you talk to him—he will soon learn to respond.

Don't have a crowd waiting at home to greet your dog as this can be overwhelming and you want him to feel secure. First introduce him to the yard while he is on his leash so he can explore his new surroundings. Show him the spot you have designated as the place where he will relieve himself and encourage him to make use of it. He may not understand at first, but if you keep to a routine and bring him to that spot numerous times throughout the day, waiting patiently there and saying "go potty," the message will become clearer each time. Be prepared for accidents in the home until he is fully housetrained and even if he already is. Nervousness and excitement contribute to accidents, and this is to be expected. Bring the dog into your home, to the room where his bed, a few toys, water, and food bowl are kept. Leave the leash on for his first walk around and then let him off the leash to familiarize himself with the room on his own, using baby gates to block him from the other rooms so he can get used to things slowly. If there are other family members for him to meet, keep things calm and allow him to approach them first.

Dog Fact

Time your new dog's arrival for when you have a few days you can be at home. He needs you to help make his transition smooth, and quality time together at the beginning builds your bond quickly.

Home Sweet Home

Everyone in your home must understand the house rules and consistently communicate them to the dog. This sends him a clear message regarding what you expect of him and communicates that they are all higher in the pack than he is. Your dog-care regime should be decided before you bring your dog home. Each family member should take it in turn to feed and walk the dog so that he understands that pleasant experiences are to be associated with each of them.

DOG PROOFING

A dog is inquisitive, especially when he is in a new situation. He doesn't know what is safe and what isn't so it is up to you to protect him by looking at your home through his sense of sight and smell.

INSIDE YOUR HOME

Electrical cords should be out of sight and reach. Tuck them behind furniture and under carpets. Drapery and blind cords should be tied up so your dog can't tug at them. Put childproof latches on cupboards that contain anything dangerous, like cleaning solutions or medication. Move anything fragile out of reach, including plants, some of which may be toxic to your dog. Anything that can be swallowed—small ornaments, buttons, coins, paperclips, socks, nylons—should be safely stored.

Make sure that your trash can has a tight-fitting lid that he won't be able to dislodge, including bathroom trash cans, which may contain dangerous items like razors. If you are using baby gates to restrict access, the bars should be close enough together that he can't get his head stuck between them. Many dogs like to drink from the toilet bowl, so keep the lid down and sanitizing flush products out.

OUTSIDE YOUR HOME

Check that any fencing is secure and that there are no holes or gaps that he could slip through or get stuck in. Remove any toxic plants or fence them in. Secure gates to a pool and prevent easy access to a garage or shed. Antifreeze smells sweet to dogs and is especially tempting, so keep it and any other hazardous items—nails, wire, pesticides, gasoline, fishing rods, and lures—out of reach.

Reward your pup for good behavior, like when he enters his crate to explore. You want to let him know the crate is a pleasant place and encourage him to see it as his own room. Dogs feel secure in their crate or "den" once they are used to it, so leave the crate's door open for the first few days until he feels safe there—a positive association with his crate will be invaluable when it comes to traveling with him later or leaving him alone for short periods of time. Too much stimulation doesn't help your dog settle in easily, so give him short periods of alone time. This also helps him understand from day one that you can't always be with him but that you will be back. When it is time for sleep, lead him to his dog bed, which should have a towel or blanket with your scent or that of his littermates to help him feel secure. A radio playing softly nearby can make him feel less alone when the rest of the house is asleep, and a few chew toys can keep him busy if the new experiences of the day haven't already tired him out.

The initiation period should be an enjoyable time in which you and your dog get to know each other and he learns to trust you, forming the foundation needed for you to understand each other.

It can take days or months for your dog to feel comfortable in his new home, with most dogs feeling at ease in about a month. Setting and following a routine are the best ways to make this happen.

BEHIND THE SIGNS

Help Your Dog Put His Right Paw Forward

Teach children that, although they may want to play with the dog, rushing at him, overly loud voices, or rough-housing send the wrong message. Instead of seeing them as playmates the dog could become afraid of them, and react with growls, nips, or bites. Other dogs in the home can provide a challenge. Introduce your new dog to his canine companion gradually, keeping both on a leash at first. Let them sniff each other; it is their way of getting to know each other, but watch for signs of fear or aggression. Make the experience as pleasant as possible with rewards and treats for good behavior, so they associate the other dog with enjoyment. Feed them separately at first, until they have become friends. Give each of them time with you. Neglecting one dog while helping the other settle in will lead to jealousy and problem behavior. Watch them carefully during the first couple of weeks, stepping in with a stern "no" when necessary. They already speak the same language; they may just need time to establish their roles.

Now that you've seen to your dog's physical comforts, it is time to look at his emotional needs. You will need to win him over and gain his trust. To do that he must know that you, and other people in the home, are the leaders. He needs to understand that he is a much-loved subordinate, not an equal, and it is an easy message for him to understand because it is the same message his mother taught him. You may be tempted to spoil him at first, thinking it will help him settle in. The reality is this sets a precedent and it is a lot harder to fix things later if you haven't started off right. A calm manner and consistent attitude communicate leadership; anything else forms the foundation for a relationship where you don't understand each other. Set house rules before you bring your dog home, so that everyone in the house knows the importance of giving your dog clear signals as to what is expected. Your dog wants to please you but he needs your help to do so and mistakes on his part are a natural way of learning what not to do. Be reasonable in your expectations and give your dog time to decipher your language and adjust to his new home. In this way your dog becomes a well-mannered family member and not a burden.

DOG SENSE

CANINE INTERACTION WITH THEIR ENVIRONMENT

Canines share our senses: they see, smell, hear, touch, and taste, but not as we do. Some senses, like hearing, are more highly developed in our dogs, while other senses, like taste, fall short of the general human experience. When we understand what the world is like from our dogs' perspective, their behavior makes more sense, and our communication with our canines is enhanced.

I SPY

How well dogs see depends on their field of view, ability to judge distances (depth perception), focusing ability (acuity), perception of motion, and color differentiation. With eyes placed on the side of their heads—an aid to peripheral vision—most dogs have a wide field of vision. This is useful when hunting and also means that hand signals in training can help ensure good communication between you and your canine. Skull shape also plays a part in determining peripheral and panoramic vision; it influences the position of the eyes, so a dog like the Pug—with his large, round head—will have narrower vision than a dog of the Labrador Retriever breed. Dogs may not be strong at judging distances or seeing detail, but they are good at detecting motion—in part thanks to that peripheral vision—which is why a dog's vision is so much better than ours when it comes to spotting a squirrel climbing a tree. Some breeds, like the Afghan Hound, were specifically bred to chase prey by sight over long distances—easy enough if their prey kept moving but much more difficult if it kept still.

Dog Fact

Dogs aren't color blind but they are underwhelmed by color; colors appear more muted and are not as easily discernible as they are to us.

Color Coded

Dogs may have an easier time spotting a blue toy in the grass, rather than a green or orange toy, since they don't recognize as many colors as we do and find some colors easier to detect than others. They also don't see stationary objects as clearly, which is why you may have an easier time finding your dog's tennis ball in the grass than he does. They make up for these sensory shortcomings with a powerful olfactory sense. If they are looking for something in the garden, their powerful snout will eventually sniff it out, regardless of color or movement.

Although it varies according to breed, age, and health, many dogs have the ability to see a hand waving from up to a mile away. A dog's vision is usually best at dusk and dawn.

Scientific studies have proven that dogs are not color blind, as was once thought, although colors appear more muted to them. They see only a limited range of colors and rely on contrast and movement, rather than color, to identify objects. Dogs have a layer in the eye that reflects light back to the receptor cells, which can give their eyes the appearance of glowing in the dark. It also makes their low-light and night vision better than ours. This, along with their skill at recognizing moving objects, are talents made use of in guide, hunting, guard, and retriever dogs.

BEHIND THE SIGNS

NOSE IN THE AIR

Your dog's sense of smell is the most perfected of his senses and research indicates that he may have used it prenatally. He uses it to explore and define his environment and can even tell time with it: strong scents indicate newness while weaker scents signal age. He gathers a lot of information about you through his nose as well, such as where you've been and how you are feeling emotionally. Scent is not just pleasant or unpleasant to a dog; it tells a story. It lets a dog know when a stranger has been sitting on his favorite chair, or the sex of the dog that peed against the traffic lights at the end of the road.

Powerful Pheromones

A dog interprets the world predominantly by smell, whereas humans use sight and sound. Olfaction, the act or process of smelling, is a dog's primary sense. Scent receptors send impulses associated with sexual and social behaviors to the dog's brain, turning pheromones—a body's scent—into a story that communicates much to the dog about the person or canine he has smelled.

Humans have about five million scent receptors inside their nose, while a dog may have over 200 million—a Beagle's nose has 300 million receptors, for example. It varies according to breed, with Bloodhounds able to identify scales of human skin shed three days past. This is due in part to the number of scent receptors in the nose but also to the mechanics of the canine nose. Their nostrils quiver as they breathe in, pulling the air—and the scent—in deeper. Air escapes through the side slits of their nose, helping to create a breeze that pulls more air and scent in. Dogs also have a nasal pocket in which strange odor molecules can be collected in order to give their receptors a better chance of identifying the smell. Additionally, a dog's refined sense of smell is heightened further thanks to the wetness of his nose; the moisture secreted by mucous glands helps capture scent particles. This acute sense of smell has been encouraged through breeding for use in hunting, policing, and search and rescue. Dogs can sniff out prey, detect contraband products such as drugs, and track missing persons.

BEHIND THE SIGNS

Follow the Nose

Sniffing helps a dog to maximize detection of odors. When sniffing, a dog disrupts his normal breathing pattern and instead uses a series of rapid, short inhalations and exhalations. This differs from breathing in that the short breaths do not exhale all of the scent, therefore allowing the dog's millions of scent receptors longer to analyze and record them. It is this that the dog uses to understand his environment: who has been there, how they were feeling, when they were there, and where they were previously.

LED BY THE NOSE

A dog's olfactory senses far surpass ours. Although their sense of sight is impressive in its ability to recognize movement, it can be considered a lesser sense. The same goes for hearing; a dog's hearing is acute and incredibly useful, but not a deal-breaker. Blind or deaf dogs can manage quite well without their sense of sight or sound. It is their nose and its superior sense of smell, above all else, that guides them.

THE DEVELOPMENT OF SENSES

Taste, touch, and smell are the first of the senses to develop in a newborn puppy. By the third week, a pup's eyes and auditory canals open so he can communicate with his mother and siblings. By the fifth week, the puppy's senses are generally fully developed and he is able to explore his environment fully by examining and sniffing everything.

TASTE, TOUCH, AND SMELL: at birth
SOUND: two to four weeks of age
SIGHT: well developed at four to five weeks of age, although eyes open earlier

LISTEN UP

Compared to people, a dog's ears are better designed to capture sound. They are highly mobile, which contributes to superior hearing. Much of what we say is just noise to our dogs—our body language tells them much more than our words do—but if they hear something interesting from their environment their ears perk up and they may tilt their head in the direction of the sound. Puppies tend to do this more frequently given their curious natures and the fact that they are still trying to understand which noises are important and which aren't.

Canines can move each ear independently, using both ears to maximize the reception of sound waves or cocking one ear to localize sound. The latter is useful when sound is coming from the front or back; when it comes from the sides a dog's ears are already in position. Dogs with hanging ears may have a slight disadvantage due to the impedance caused by the ear canals being covered. Perked ears have an unencumbered ear opening and are generally more mobile, able to turn easily to the direction of sound. Regardless of breed, all dogs can hear a wider range of frequencies at a greater distance than the human ear and can hear certain pitches that are inaudible to us. Of course, this won't be news to many dog owners; common is the story of a quiet evening at home disrupted by the barks of the dog. The reason for this isn't clear until the doorbell rings minutes later to announce a visitor that the dog was already well aware was on the way.

TOUCH AND TASTE

One of the first sensations your dog experiences is the touch of his mother licking him, and touch remains an important sense from day one. Even before their sense of sight develops, pups are able to find their mother and connect with her by using the sensory receptors in their face. "Vibrissae" are the whiskers your dog has above his eyes, on his muzzle, and below his jaw. They are touch-sensitive and can detect airflow, letting the dog know about any nearby objects, even if he can't see them. Most dogs enjoy being patted and stroked, but some dogs—if they haven't been handled much from birth and were not socialized properly—may be nervous about being touched because it is unfamiliar. Breeds who were bred to chase game through the countryside, running through wild terrain, may be less responsive to touch. Sensitivity varies, but all dogs have touch-sensitive nerve endings located throughout their body.

Dog Fact

If you are puzzled by your dog's behavior, keep in mind that his worldview is dictated by senses that work differently from ours. What is he trying to tell you?

 $\mathcal{Dog\ Fact}$

The verdict is still out, but recent medical tests indicate that professionally trained dogs may be capable of detecting certain medical conditions, like melanoma, in humans.

Most dogs aren't picky and will eat anything they can get their mouths around. They can differentiate between sweet, sour, bitter, and salty, but don't have a strong sense of taste. They defer to their sense of smell instead; sometimes that means the smellier the better. Most of a dog's taste buds are found around the tip of his tongue, which he may not get much of an opportunity to use as dogs often gulp first, and don't bother with the niceties associated with a refined palate.

WONDERING ABOUT WHISKERS?

Your dog's whiskers don't just add to his facial features; they are also sophisticated touch receptors. Known as "vibrissae," these thick hairs were some of the first hairs that your pup grew and they helped him to get to know the world around him. They continue to act as a tour guide because, as your dog moves around, his whiskers sense airflow, and vibrate to communicate the presence of nearby objects. Located above his eyes, on his muzzle, and below his jaw, these whiskers look like long, thick facial hairs and are in fact valuable canine tools.

CANINE COMMUNICATION

HOW BODY LANGUAGE CONVEYS MESSAGES

*D*ogs are very social animals that easily communicate their feelings; they just do it a little differently than people do. At one point, long before language evolved, humans communicated in much the same way: we relied on our bodies to communicate. Today our language is spoken and, although our canines use vocal communication, their language has remained primarily non-verbal, yet no less expressive. Facial expression, body language, and posture effectively convey meaning, once we know how to interpret the messages. Although extremes, such as threatening postures, may be easily interpreted, the subtleties aren't always as clear unless you understand the signals that comprise canine body language: starting from a dog's ears to his tail.

A dog's ears are a lot more expressive than ours, with a wide variety of shapes and sizes depending on breed: the French Bulldog has what is known as bat ears; the Basset Hound has dropped ears; while the Basenji has pricked ears. This variation means that some dogs can hear and communicate more with their ears than others. The "alert" signal is indicated with ears raised high and pointed toward whatever has got the dog's attention. It communicates interest, "What's that? I want to know more," or aggression, "I feel threatened." Depending on the breed, a dog may communicate submissiveness with ears that either stick out at the sides of his head, or with ears that are completely flattened. If the ears are just pulled back slightly the message is different yet again and communicates friendliness, while ears that are held naturally are a sign that the dog feels relaxed.

Canine Ears Speak

A dog's ears are part of the vocabulary that makes up canine body language. Depending on their size and shape they can help to communicate many emotions, from contented to fearful. They have also been classified into different descriptive groups, for example:

BAT EAR: Set fairly far apart they are wide at the base, large in proportion to the head, and are carried erect and forward-facing, like the ears of a Chihuahua.

BLUNT-TIPPED EAR: Also known as round-tipped because of their shape, as seen on the Chow Chow.

COCKED EAR: The tip of the ear turns forward slightly, as seen on the Pitbull or Shetland Sheepdog. Also known as semi-crop, semi-prick, or tipped ears.

DROPPED EAR: Sometimes called folded, pendant, or pendulous. The ears hang down from the side of the head, like a Norfolk Terrier's ears.

PRICK EAR: The tips of the ears can be rounded or pointed and the ears stand up stiffly, as seen on the German Shepherd.

ROSE EAR: Small and thin, with the upper edge of the ear curving over and back, like the ears of a Greyhound.

BEHIND THE SIGNS

Dog Fact

By understanding how our canines "speak" we can interact with them confidently and protect them when needed.

It's a Dog Thing

Housetraining accidents are not always what they seem. A submissive dog may sometimes urinate when confronted with a more dominant member of the pack, which could be you or someone else in your household. Most dogs outgrow submissive urination and the best way to handle it is to ignore it; instead, lead your dog to the place where he is permitted to relieve himself and encourage him to do his business there.

The messages conveyed by a dog's eyes are sometimes overlooked in discussions of body language, yet the power of a held gaze or a wandering eye to communicate plays its part. Like people, an unconfident dog may avoid eye contact when you look at him. His look says he's not sure about interacting with you or that he is submissive. A direct gaze can be either threatening or friendly depending on the intensity of the look; given in a relaxed manner it means the dog is feeling friendly, while an intense stare indicates the dog is feeling aggressive. Slowly look away from this dog. By doing so you are speaking their language; it is what other dogs would do to communicate they are not a threat.

A dog that looks at you out of the corner of his eyes means business, and is sending a serious warning of his intent to be aggressive. Don't mistake this for the relaxed sideways glance as you walk by; the latter is a sign of curiosity and—unlike the aggressive sideways look—is less intense, with the whites of the eyes less visible. The size of your dog's eyes in a given situation is also telling: eyes that appear larger than usual can indicate high alertness due to stress or aggression; eyes that appear smaller than usual can indicate pain and discomfort; and eyes that are squinting may indicate submissiveness, although this can also be a sign of aggression—a key indicator here is the intensity with which the dog holds his gaze.

THE BIG PICTURE

Familiarity with how a dog uses his facial expressions, body language, and posture to communicate is the first step in learning canine language.

ALERT: Something has caught the dog's attention, but he doesn't yet know if it is threatening. He may exhibit aggressive body language as a protective measure, appearing taller, with ears perked up. His tail may also be elevated. His hackles may be up, his mouth will usually be closed or opened slightly with teeth covered, and his gaze will be focused.

AGGRESSIVE: Dogs act aggressively when they feel threatened, either out of fear or because their dominance is being challenged. Regardless of the reason, they will stand tall in an attempt to seem bigger and more intimidating. There are variations amongst breeds, but generally the dog's ears and tail will be up, and the hair on the tail fluffed. The hair along the dog's neck and back may be up as well, his ears will point forward slightly, his teeth will be visible, he may snap his jaw, and his neck will be arched. His stare is direct and intense, possibly with narrowed eyes. He may lean forward, ready to lunge.

ANXIOUS OR FEARFUL: The dog will do his best to appear as small as possible, with legs bent, body hunched, tail down or tucked between his rear legs, and ears flat. His body will be tense or may tremble, he may avert his eyes or yawn to show he is not a threat or he may not be able to take his eyes off whatever it is that is causing his fear or stress.

DOMINANT: A tall and confident stance with weight balanced evenly, or leaning forward slightly in a "back off" gesture. Generally the mouth is closed (unlike the aggressive mouth position) and eye contact is direct and assertive. This body language says "I'm higher in the pecking order," and is not bullying behavior; it is simply the dog stating a fact. This can lead to aggressive behavior if the dog feels challenged.

FRIENDLY, EAGER, OR PLAYFUL: No tenseness in the body, which is held in a natural position. His ears will be perked, eyes wide, mouth slightly open with teeth covered, and his tail will wag. A playful dog may pant excitably, jump about, run in circles, invite you to play by raising and wriggling his rear (known as a "play bow"), or by pawing the air.

SUBMISSIVE: Similar to that of the anxious dog, although submissiveness is not necessarily caused by fear or a lack of confidence. In healthy situations, it is simply the dog recognizing that he is subordinate to his pack leader. He may lower his body to the ground, lie on his back, urinate, or lick and nuzzle the person or the other dog. His ears may be turned up in a gesture of submissive trust or they will be flattened, he will avert his gaze, and his teeth may be exposed with his lips turned up in a submissive grin. His tail will generally be tucked between his rear legs. If faced with aggression, he may try to turn it off with gestures that are meant to placate and relieve tension, such as looking away, sneezing, or yawning.

Just as with people, the position of the mouth speaks about current mood and intentions. Aggression is the most commonly recognized, when the lips are pulled back and up to expose teeth. Less easily understood is the "grin," which, because the teeth are exposed and the lips are turned up, can be confused with an aggressive look, but communicates that the dog is feeling very submissive. Dogs also show submissiveness with a closed mouth, or by licking the person or animal they are interacting with. A yawn may not mean that the dog is tired; it is a canine signal used to placate a threat.

 Dog Fact

An exaggerated yawn is often used to release tension and could be a signal that the dog feels intimidated.

BEHIND THE SIGNS

You're Invited to . . . Play

When a dog gives you the play bow—forelegs are on the ground with his hind legs extended so that his rear sticks up—he's asking you to play. It may look like the dog is stretching, although his tail is also wagging and he may wriggle his rear. It is a common behavior among dogs and is an important communication tool, letting people and other dogs know that he is relaxed and feeling playful. Whenever you see your canine giving you a play bow, you can be sure that fun times are ahead for you both.

Dog Fact

A dog that doesn't understand a message from his owner may tilt his head to one side and raise his eyebrows quizzically in much the same way as people. Even a dog's forehead speaks: he may wrinkle or straighten it to indicate uncertainty or confusion.

When You Look at My Leash I Know It's Time for a Walk

Research has shown that not only can you tell what your dog is communicating by his body language, he does the same by observing you. Social cognition in dogs—their ability to comprehend the signals of others—has been studied for decades and is evident in their response to a person's pointed finger, tilted head, or a glance toward an object. Animals are generally quite good at interpreting signals within their own species; however, scientists have shown that the dog's level of perception extends beyond canines. Daniel J. Povinelli, a psychologist at the University of Southwestern Louisiana, tested chimpanzees' responses to cues given by people and a team led by Robert Hare of Harvard University ran the same test on dogs. Canines came out ahead, and have even been shown to have a level of social cognition better than that of a three-year-old child.

Dogs don't often look directly into another canine's eyes because in their language this sends a threatening message. They have learned that it is different when communicating with people and that it can be pleasant to look directly at them.

Dog tails tell a tale about the dog's attitude and intentions. A relaxed dog holds his tail naturally, while a dog on alert holds his tail stiff and higher than normal. A threatening dog may give warning by moving a stiff tail that is held high back and forth, known as "flagging" his tail. The intensity accompanied by the action is key. A wagging tail held tensely is a potential threat, while a gently or exuberantly wagging tail is friendly. Breed must also be taken into consideration. A tail tucked between the rear legs can often indicate submissiveness. However, breeds like the whippet have tails that do this naturally. Dogs with shorter tails can't always make their feelings known as forcibly as dogs with longer and more expressive tails.

AGGRESSIVE

WHAT IT MEANS
"Don't mess with me." This dog may be dominant or fearful; the dominant dog will meet any challenge, the fearful dog may be bluffing or considers a good offense to be the best defense.

WHAT TO DO
Obedience classes are imperative for dogs that show aggressive tendencies and an animal behaviorist may be necessary. Fights will happen when this behavior is directed at another dog who does not respond submissively. If this behavior is directed toward a person, retreat is best; back away slowly without making eye contact, as the latter could be seen as a challenge.

SUBMISSIVE

WHAT IT MEANS
"I'm no threat," or "I recognize your leadership." Submissive behavior is meant to either appease more dominant pack members or show them respect and affection.

WHAT TO DO
This behavior is only a problem if it is excessive, in which case you can lower yourself to your dog's level on the floor and let him come to you, and then give him positive reinforcement. Don't yell or look at these dogs directly in the eyes, as this may reinforce the behavior. Obedience training classes will build confidence.

CONFIDENT AND RELAXED

WHAT IT MEANS
"All's well." This dog is comfortable in his environment and everything about his body language underlines that fact. Whether he's just been out for a long walk or just been fed, he is satisfied and content and will probably be happy to spend a few quiet moments in his own company.

WHAT TO DO
Enjoy it. This is an approachable and content dog.

EXCITED AND PLAYFUL

WHAT IT MEANS
"I'm looking forward to this," or "It's time for a game."

WHAT TO DO
This is a perfect time to build your bond through play, but if you are unable to play with your dog at this time make sure he has toys to keep him occupied and room to run.

The Universal Language

The Expression of the Emotions in Man and Animals by Charles Darwin (1872) encouraged an interest in ethology, the study of animal behavior. In it, Darwin wrote about the universal use of common expressions: "the young and the old of widely different races, both with man and animals, express the same state of mind by the same movements."

Dog Fact

In general, dogs will make themselves look big (aggressive, confident, alert), small (submissive, afraid), or will hold themselves naturally (friendly, relaxed, content).

Communication also comes via a dog's coat and posture. Dogs in stressful situations tend to shed more than usual, and raised hair indicates arousal due to fear, anger, anxiety, or excitement. A scared dog will try to appear smaller, just as a submissive dog will. They may get as close to the ground as possible. A dominant dog, a dog on alert, or an aggressive dog will try to look larger. He will stand tall, even on tiptoes in some cases, and hold his neck and head high with his weight balanced evenly or slightly leaning forward in the "ready for action" pose. A relaxed dog holds himself naturally, not trying to hide or intimidate. A dog who is not sure if there is a threat may investigate, holding most of his weight on his back legs. His posture says, "I'm not sure about this, but I'm going to check it out and if it is something threatening at least I can get out of here fast."

MIXED MESSAGES

It is easy to misread the signs and interpret non-verbal language incorrectly, but regularly observing your dog as he interacts with you and others will make the translation easier. A common error is to mistake the submissive grin for aggression. In both cases the dog's lips will turn up and his front teeth will be exposed, but the meaning differs. An aggressive dog is using his teeth to intimidate; a submissive dog is saying the exact opposite by signaling that he is not a threat and won't cause any problems. Not understanding the message can have serious consequences for the dog, which is why it is important to look at more than just the mouth to understand the message. All aspects of body language—facial expressions, ear set, tail carriage, body language, and posture—combine to make up the message, and translate its meaning.

GROWLING AS COMMUNICATION

THE MEANING BEHIND THE MESSAGE

WHAT YOU HEAR

A low rumbling, throaty sound, varying in intensity depending on situation.

WHAT IT MEANS

"Back away!" The dog perceives a threat, real or not, and growling is his defense signal, warning of his readiness to act aggressively.

WHAT TO KNOW

Growling is the language of aggression. The threat level of a growl is dependent on the dog and the situation; used in play it may be a mock growl, but when used as a threat it can be very serious. Dogs growl to repel the person or canine who threatens them, their pack, their territory, or possessions. The pitch and tone of the growl can make both large and small dogs intimidating, which is exactly its purpose. This behavior may come from any dog, whether overly confident or passive in temperament. When pushed, even the latter can react aggressively, starting with a warning growl.

Content Dogs Are Not Frequent Growlers

It is easy to make excuses for dogs when they growl at other people or canines. Owners may say "He's just scared," or "You startled him; he'll stop growling in a minute." This can lead to escalated problem behavior and entirely avoidable acts of aggression, such as lunging and biting. Obedience training helps dogs to be well-mannered companions and socialization helps them respond positively to people, animals, and different situations—giving them less reason to react with a growl.

Growling is most often the lightning before the thunder, so the best thing you can do when growled at is to heed your instinct to walk away. Say "no" firmly, while calmly and slowly backing away with your arms at your side. Don't make eye contact, which canines may interpret as a threat. Give the dog space, let him know you heard and listened to his message. It doesn't matter if the dog is submissive or dominant: the submissive dog may feel fearful; the dominant dog may feel forceful. Either way, the end result can be the same: a warning growl followed by aggression.

Manage situations with your dog to avoid aggression. Keep him on a leash when in public and avoid any dog who, through his vocalization or body language, is exhibiting aggression. If your dog is attacked by another dog, don't try to interrupt them. Although injuries are a possibility, their fight won't last long and trying to get between them may only get them more excited, and will put you at risk. Avoid rough games like tug of war that can lead to overstimulation and encourage growling.

Dog Fact

Mock growling during play is not uncommon, and is generally meant as a lighthearted warning. Rough play and competition can escalate things quickly, turning what was playful into a more serious warning. Avoid tug-of-war style games and, if play gets too intense, stop and allow your dog to calm down.

King Complex

Some dogs are lap sitters and when dogs are subordinate to their people this does not pose a problem. If the dog is not subordinate, however, he may act possessively, growling at anyone who approaches. He is king and you are the throne and, as the dominant pack member, he sees it as his role to control the movement of others by deterring them with growling and possibly even more aggressive behavior. These dogs need to relearn their place through consistent leadership and training by their owners.

GREEN MEANS GO

Pitch is important when translating a dog's growl, although this is best done after the fact. A higher-pitched growl is the least threatening, meaning "leave me alone." It is the amber traffic light of growls, and gives warning. A medium-pitched growl is more threatening and communicates the seriousness of the dog's intentions if his warning growl is not heeded right away, while a belly growl is low-pitched and most intimidating of all—it is the green traffic light of growls, given when the dog is ready to bite.

Dog Fact

Dogs that are injured or in pain may growl when the affected area is touched.

Let children and visitors in the home know that rough games and teasing are not to be permitted. The dog may not understand that their intention is fun rather than threatening.

Obedience training, of course, can't be overemphasized: it teaches dominant dogs their place; it can help fearful dogs be less fearful, so they feel less threatened in general; and it gives you a common language, so that you can communicate with your dog in difficult situations. Dogs who recognize their owner as the leader are less territorial because they recognize that it is not their job to defend the pack. Possessiveness in your dog can also lead to growling and aggression. Although not to be encouraged, it is still best not to interrupt your dog when he is eating, or try to take something—his chew toys, your slippers—directly from his mouth. In the latter case, train him to give it to you on command or, failing that, try to distract him so he releases the object, rather than starting a tug of war between you. It goes without saying than any physical punishment is wrong. It can also cause a dog to lash out, just as screaming at him can. From a dog's perspective he is being threatened and growling is the warning given before he retaliates. Listen to him. A dog's growl may be worse than his bite, but why put it to the test?

BEHIND THE SIGNS

Increase Your Canine Vocabulary

Many hounds use a sound known as "baying," which is like a bark but longer in duration and of deeper tones. As hunting dogs, they use it to announce to pack members that prey has been sighted. Some dogs, like the Basenji, are known as the "barkless dog" because they convey excitement with an undulating vocalization similar in style to a yodel. This is due to the shape of their larynx, which differs from the vast majority of canine species.

WHINING AS COMMUNICATION

ARE YOU THERE?

WHAT YOU HEAR

A nasal cry varying in pitch and volume, which may be accompanied by restless movement.

WHAT IT MEANS

Frustration or "I want attention."

WHAT TO DO

Look at the situation. Is your dog hungry, cold, or does he need to relieve himself? Or is he looking for attention? If the former, respond. If the latter, ignore so as not to reinforce the behavior.

Whining is a communication that starts early in life. Pups use it to tell their mother there is a need to be met, and she quickly responds. Although it starts as an automatic reaction to something lacking—companionship, food, comfort—the quick response he receives tells the puppy that whining gets results. Your dog carries this behavior into his relationship with you. Every time he whines he is "saying" something, but you will need to understand his whining to know if it is a valid communication, or simply attention-seeking behavior.

A dog new to your home may have a good reason for whining, especially at night. He is alone, possibly for the fist time since leaving the litter, and is in a strange environment. He is unsettled and perhaps overstimulated. Check that your dog is okay by going to him, but don't say much; give him eye contact or cuddle him. In this case he just needs to know you are there and anything further teaches him whining means a big payday. Your presence for a few minutes is enough to let your dog know that you hear him and that you care. Preventative measures may make night-whiners feel more secure: a towel or blanket with your scent or that of his littermates can reassure him; a ticking clock tucked into a pillow can be soothing for your dog.

If your dog is an infrequent whiner you can generally interpret his message as real. He may be uncomfortable or he may be feeling poorly. Look for the cause and alleviate it. Is there anything frightening him? Does he need to relieve himself outside? This should be the only acceptable attention-seeking whine you recognize and it is easy to spot as your dog will often be at the door when he whines, communicating that he needs to get out fast. Is he too cold or hot, thirsty or bored? Check the temperature, check that he has water and chew toys. Does he look less alert than usual? If so he may not be feeling well, in which case the whining will persist even after you go to him. Check for a fever and look for signs of injury, and contact your veterinarian if the whining persists.

Whining that ceases with your presence and starts up again as you leave is likely attention-seeking behavior and, hard as it is, you should ignore it. If your dog is a whiner note what you are doing when the whining starts. Is it primarily when you leave the room, or when you sit down to dinner or a television show? If so, teach your dog that the squeaky wheel doesn't always get the grease. When you give him the attention he is

BEHIND THE SIGNS

Quiet Behavior: 1 Whining: 0

Reward quiet behavior. If we only pay attention to our dogs when they are noisy that sends a clear message as to what gets results. Every interaction your dog has with you is a lesson, and practice makes perfect. Help your dog to be successful by reinforcing good behavior. Give him attention, treats, walks, playtime, petting—but only when he has been quiet for at least five seconds. This teaches him that silence has its own—and better— rewards: positive attention.

WHINE NOT?

Don't give your dog anything to whine about. Spend plenty of time with him each day so you can be confident that any attention-seeking whining is excessive and unnecessary. If he has regular quality time with you, such as walks, playtime, chew toys, and a routine, he will be less likely to whine out of boredom or neediness. Other types of whining behavior may include:

APPEASEMENT

This is a natural canine reaction to a perceived threat, often seen in dogs that lack confidence. Obedience training can build confidence and decrease this type of whining.

EXCITEMENT

Dogs that whine when greeting people or other dogs are generally overstimulated. Keep greetings short and simple, and always use a calm, matter-of-fact voice. Eventually your dog will follow your cue but in the meantime you may want to distract him when whining behavior starts by giving him a command such as "sit" or "down" to calm him.

BEHIND THE SIGNS

looking for, you have just had a training session with him and he has learned that whining is self-rewarding. It gets the result he was after—your attention—and he will escalate the behavior in the future. Don't scold him, as even negative attention is still attention. His behavior needs to be unlearned. By ignoring him he should learn that whining won't work. He will get the message, as long as you send it consistently and clearly. It may seem cold-hearted, but it is easier to stop this behavior in the beginning rather than reinforce and escalate it through your response. Be there when needed, but learn to differentiate between following your dog's every wish and direction, and true need. You should be training him, not the other way around. By responding each and every time you are doing him no favors; he learns that he is the one who controls your relationship and this results in a pushy, demanding dog and problem behavior. Your dog needs your leadership. Without it, you give him something real to whine about.

Solitary Whining

If your dog whines only when he is alone at home, without anyone around, then it may be a sign of separation anxiety (see p. 123). This is not attention-seeking behavior; it is a very real anxiety that your dog experiences and that can lead to destructive behavior. If this is the case, your dog will show other symptoms, such as scratching at doors and windows, pacing, anxiety whenever you leave the house, and overly effusive greetings when you return.

 ## Dog Fact

If your dog has never been a whiner but suddenly starts, pay attention: he may be injured or sick. Gently check him, looking for physical signs to explain the behavior. If there is no easily discernible answer and the whining persists, contact your veterinarian.

BARKING AS COMMUNICATION

IT'S MORE THAN JUST NOISE

WHAT YOU HEAR

A short, sharp cry. Duration, tone, and rhythm vary according to the message.

WHAT IT MEANS

Greeting or excitement: "Hello!" or "This is fun!"
Anxiety: "I'm lonely!"
Alarm: "I heard something you should know about!"
Warning: "Don't come any closer!"
Attention: "Pay attention to me!"

Barking is not bad behavior; it is simply canine behavior. Dogs bark, in part because during the domestication process vocalization was one of the traits encouraged through breeding: it made for good guard and hunting dogs. As a result, it is the most common of dog noises and an all-purpose form of canine communication. Persistent barking, however, can be a problem. Key to dealing with problem behavior is to look beyond the behavior to the reason why. Understand the language of barking and you will have a better understanding of your dog, what triggers nuisance barking, and how to discourage it.

BEHIND THE SIGNS

Barking Up the Wrong Tree

Excessive barking is usually a result of owner mismanagement. Does your dog bark persistently when you are on the telephone or watching television? If you reprimand him you are rewarding him. Dogs learn what we teach them; if your dog learns that nuisance barking gets him what he wants—in this case, your attention— he will remember it next time. When your dog barks excessively, look at the context to determine if his behavior is a natural reaction to a stressful situation, such as being left alone for long periods of time, or if it is an inappropriate behavior that he plays out to get attention.

Duration, tone, and rhythm all provide clues to your dog's message, as does the situation that triggers the barking. Most important in deciphering the message is your dog's body language. A dog's bark may initially seem to vary little, but it becomes rapidly clear just how many different messages the multipurpose bark can communicate.

EXCITEMENT AND GREETING

This is usually a short, sharp bark. Used to express eagerness, this is often heard when you arrive home or when your dog is at play. If your dog becomes overexcited then make your return home less of an occasion. Ignore your dog totally until the barking lessens, then praise him immediately by saying "good, quiet," and give him attention in the form of a game or walk. If it is a game that has him overexcited, change to a more calming activity or take a time-out. Again, as soon as the barking subsides, praise him. Do this each and every time so your dog knows what types of behavior gets the reaction he wants, and which ones don't.

Dog Fact

Understanding the message and retraining by reward when needed is the most effective way of communicating with your dog. Dogs bark—some breeds more than others—but with care, consistency, and training, excessive barking should not be a problem.

ANXIETY

Persistent barking may occur when the dog is stressed, for example, if left alone for long periods of time. Dogs are social animals and should never be left isolated for too long. They need companionship just as they need regular exercise and mental stimulation. Providing they get this, they have less reason to bark excessively.

The Warning Bark

Fear-based barking translates to "stay away," and should always be heeded. The dog may normally be submissive or dominant but, when frightened, may react with aggression as a defense reflex, regardless of his normal temperament. This is initially communicated through a low-pitched warning bark that may progress to non-stop, inhale-exhale panic barking. Frightened dogs can be uncontrollable; understand that the dog is saying "stay away," and act on that.

ALARM OR WARNING

An alarm bark is generally a burst of two or three sharp barks with short pauses between them. A ringing telephone, a doorbell, a neighbor's car starting; any noise that the dog wants to draw your attention to may trigger it. A warning bark may start out similar to an alarm bark and get lower in tone and more rapid, and may include growling, as what the dog hears or sees as a threat moves closer into his territory. Obedience training can help dominant dogs to be less territorial and can increase confidence in submissive dogs, leading to less fear-based barking.

ATTENTION-SEEKING

Usually two or three barks, gradually becoming more persistent and often accompanied by an action. Your dog may nudge his food bowl and bark to let you know he is ready for his dinner, or if his chew toy has rolled under the couch he may stand facing the couch, barking to get your assistance. Respond when appropriate, for example, if your dog is frustrated because he can't reach his toy, but if his attention-seeking behavior becomes excessive then ignore it each and every time. Pay your dog no attention until the barking stops and then praise him by saying "good, quiet." Behaviors that bring pleasant results tend to be repeated, whereas behaviors that bring on consistent unpleasant results, like being ignored, are usually not repeated.

CONSISTENT RESPONSE

Dogs vocalize their emotions, just as people do. When we understand what they are saying, we're able to respond appropriately, setting a pattern for the barking to subside. Conversely, responding inappropriately sets a precedent for problem barking.

Dog Fact

A bark accompanied by a wagging tail means "let's play," while a bark accompanied by a tail sitting straight up and fluffed is a clear message to back away. Pay attention to your dog's vocalization and the accompanying body language as it completes the message and makes the meaning clear.

HOWLING AS COMMUNICATION

THE CANINE CALLING CARD

WHAT YOU HEAR

A low-pitched and loud sustained cry. Your dog's head will be back, nose pointing straight up, with his mouth wide open.

WHAT IT MEANS

The howl is a contact and reunion call among pack members. Dogs howl to attract attention, either by initiating the howl or responding to it: "I am here. Where are you?" A dog that howls when he hears a sound like an emergency vehicle or musical instrument is instinctively responding to the pitch those sounds carry.

WHAT TO DO

Some dogs will howl, and in normal circumstances this should not be a problem. If however, the behavior and duration become too frequent there are steps you can take to keep your dog, and neighbors, happy.

Your dog has a voice and should be able to use it, provided it is in moderation. Through it, you are better able to translate what your dog is feeling, and in the case of howling this might be: loneliness, camaraderie, a need to connect, or excitement. This vocalization is one aspect to understanding canine language, and the reasons behind their behavior.

The howl can be the call of the lonely looking for its pack and, despite its plaintive sound, it can also communicate excitement at a find, particularly in dogs of the hunting breed. The Beagle, for example, was bred specifically to encourage this vocalization, used as a sound alert. His job was to run ahead of hunters after prey and to howl to help the hunters follow his trail to reach their catch. The howl is still an integral part of some hunting breeds, but like all language it has evolved, and now may simply mean "I'm over here, c'mon!" The dog may not have hunters on horseback trying to follow him, but the howl remains a way to announce his whereabouts.

There are also working breeds, like the Siberian Husky, who bark little but have a propensity to howl. It makes sense because these dogs are very pack-oriented and were initially bred to travel long distances, so they would need a way to contact other pack members who might be spread out over a large area. The behavior is instinctive amongst many canines, passed down through their wolf ancestors who are thought to have used howling for a number of reasons: to make contact with their pack members, just as dogs do; to strengthen the camaraderie within their pack; and to confuse rival packs—the volume and changing tone and pitches of a wolf pack howling together made it difficult for rivals to determine their numbers.

🐾 *Dog Fact*

You are part of your dog's pack, so when apart he may howl in an attempt to make contact with you.

Dog Fact

The howl can be heard for many miles around, depending on weather conditions.

In which situations will your dog be likely to howl? If your neighbors are complaining, it is likely happening when you're not home. In this case the situation should improve if the dog is given some companionship, either through pet-sitters, dog walkers, or doggy daycare. Your dog's problem behavior is his way of making contact when he is lonely for long periods of time, saying, "I'm here. Where are you?" Some dogs howl when they hear a siren or other high-pitched sound, or in response to another dog. Some dogs howl when they hear the people members of their pack sing, just as wolves would join together in a chorus of howling. It is the dog's way of joining in on the camaraderie and showing they belong within the pack. In either case, it is not generally a problem, as their howling should stop when the sound trigger does. For dogs prone to the occasional howl you can distract them to stop it from continuing or train them to respond to "quiet," but you can't get rid of the ingrained behavior totally. The melodic howl is natural to some dogs and, in moderation, is music to the ears of many dog owners.

Canine Calling Card

A howl is a cry of long duration that sweeps through different pitches, allowing it to travel great distances. In wolf packs it is a way of giving their location to other pack members, who may have separated during the hunt. It is also used as a warning, to discourage rival pack members from coming into their territory. This long-distance communication triggers a response from other wolves and is not just powerful, it is practical. Each howl is individually recognizable, so if a lone wolf sends out a call to his pack and an unfamiliar howl is the response he knows to avoid that area.

PACK DYNAMICS

IN THE WILD AND IN YOUR HOME

When wild dogs learned not to bite the hand that fed them, domestication of the species quickly followed. Gradually this brought change in all shapes and sizes—Poodles to St. Bernards have since been bred—yet common to all is the link they share to their wolf and feral dog ancestors: pack animal behavior.

To speak your dog's language you must understand pack dynamics and how it contributes to the happiness and stability of your dog and the type of relationship you will have together. In the wild the dog pack was a means of saving energy, as hunting was easier in a group than going it alone. A pecking order was recognized within the pack, with the leader or alpha dog at the top of the hierarchy. The alpha dog made all decisions and the other members of the pack respected his authority. Today domestic dogs have no need to hunt for food but they remain hardwired to live as pack animals, with the modern pack consisting of the people and animals in their life. Just as their ancestors did, dogs continue to need social order and to know who their pack leader is. A lack of leadership results in an unhappy and anxious dog. In these situations the pack dynamic is off and you and your dog are not communicating.

 Dog Fact

A dog's social status is, rather unusually, established early in life, but circumstance may change his position, including the move to your home. At this point some canines look for opportunity to establish themselves as higher in the pecking order than their new pack members, your family. Start as you mean to go on, with caring yet firm leadership from day one.

BEHIND THE SIGNS

It's All in the Attitude

The alpha is not the leader because he is the strongest, meanest member of the pack, nor is the submissive pack member necessarily the physically weakest. True alpha leadership is about attitude and is recognized by dogs because it is how their mother was with them: firm yet gentle, and always consistent. It is the basis for mutual respect and communication between you and your canine.

He doesn't know what is expected of him or why he is rewarded sometimes and not others. As pack animals, their instincts dictate that those who set the rules are higher-ranking. If your dog is allowed to do whatever he likes this tells him that you are his subordinate. He may step into the leadership gap, assuming alpha status, and the result can be a very difficult dog to live with—one who doesn't listen, is destructive, and can be aggressive. Establishment of the people in your dog's pack as higher in the pecking order is crucial to the training of your dog. This is achieved through consistency in training and is earned when your dog understands your expectations and learns to respect limits imposed on his activities.

BEST INTENTIONS

Some owners, particularly in the case of rescue dogs, excuse problem behavior and overcompensate for what they think their dog may have experienced in the past. They provide no leadership and let their dog do as he will because, after what he may have experienced, they feel he is owed. Although their intentions are good, their actions are not a kindness to their canines. For example, it can be heartbreaking to see a dog react fearfully and aggressively to an innocently raised arm, as some dogs who have been abused do. In these cases, the dog is exhibiting a conditioned response, based on fear. Instead of accepting the problem behavior, shouldn't we try to help the dog get over this rather than allow him to feel threatened? Wouldn't it be a gift for the dog to learn that a raised hand no longer means danger, but could be the start to a game of frisbee? For this, the dog needs a pack leader to guide him, reconditioning him through training. Dogs don't dwell on the past. They may have conditioned responses to certain things, but as long as they feel safe in their current situation they are willing, with your help, to move forward as happy and stable companions.

Other owners may explain their lack of leadership as a desire for their dog to be a dog. They mistake their dog's bad behavior as individualism, and question their right to change it. However, discipline and boundaries are part of what shapes a canine's behavior. In the wild, the higher-ranking pack members begin early to teach the cubs discipline. Rules are enforced, to the benefit of the

entire pack. Playtime has its place, but the older dogs dictate when this is and don't back down, as people so often do. Pups are taught to show submissive body language to those of higher status, as a sign of affection and recognition. The young are taught to respond to commands immediately, something that keeps them safe from the dangers of the wild. These pups quickly understand that rules must be followed and have been given the tools for social order and harmony within the pack—a lesson every dog needs to be safe and happy.

Dog Fact

Your dog's ancestors, the wolf, lived in family packs of generally three to a dozen members. Your dog's pack behavior has been inherited and is an integral part of canine behavior.

CANINE TO CANINE

INTERACTION WITH OTHER DOGS

a *vital element in a dog's development is the good canine communication skills learned through play and interaction with other dogs of all ages. Play amongst puppies of the same age teaches when the "play bite" has become less play and more bite and adult dogs ensure that the maturing pups know that more adult behavior is expected of them.*

Dogs that do not get this interaction are at a social disadvantage; they may not know how to speak fluent canine if they are never with other dogs, particularly if they were separated from their litter too young. As a result, they may have difficulty in reading the signals from other dogs—aggression or deference for example. They may also be targets of aggressive behavior if they have never learned how to "tell" other canines that they are not a threat.

PLAYING NICE

In healthy play between dogs there should be a lot of give and take. Let loose at the dog park, dogs may tear around playing chase and, as long as the dog being chased becomes chaser occasionally, this is all in good fun. If not, the game may have switched from playful to hassling. If your dog is involved and you are unsure if the play has become bullying, you can test this by holding onto the collar of the dog who is doing the chasing or, in other play, seems to be consistently winning. If the "losing" dog runs toward him to continue play then all is well. Play amongst canines can sometimes look like fighting; however, dogs make this distinction through signals, including the "play bow," where one dog lowers his front half to the ground. His tail will wag loosely, his mouth will be open, and his

Play between pups of the same age becomes rougher as they mature and may resemble fighting, but dogs easily communicate with each other through the "play bow" that it is all in fun.

tongue will be exposed—clear signs to the other dog, if he chooses to accept the invitation, that what follows is play. Turid Rugaas, an expert on canine behavior and body language, states that dogs communicate calming signals to others in everyday interactions. A dog who licks their lips, yawns, circles the other dog, or sniffs the ground in a distracted way may be using calming signals to diffuse any aggression or fearfulness that rough play may have triggered.

 Dog Fact

If many of the adult dogs at the local dog park seem to be "picking" on a particular older pup then chances are good that the pup is being rude in canine terms, and drawing their communal attention.

Family Matters

Dogs first learn to correctly interact with other dogs through their relationship with their mother and littermates. Their mother may use a quick muzzle grasp to discipline them when needed and their littermates let them know when play has become too rough by stopping the game momentarily. The intensity of play can escalate quickly but it can be ended just as sharply by the signal of a playmate, teaching both dogs how they can collectively regulate the games that they play.

Although canines can be strict disciplinarians, a trait ingrained in them from when it was necessary for the survival of the dog pack, younger pups are generally allowed a lot of freedom during play, even leaping on and bumping into adult dogs. This changes as a pup reaches adolescence and moves into adulthood. At about six to nine months old, the canine groups that a pup circulates in will expect him to begin putting away puppyish behavior and the older dogs will let him know with a growl or a snap whenever they consider his behavior inappropriate. No longer is it okay to crawl all over adult dogs and any assertive behavior—such as the placing of paws across the shoulder of an older dog—will be promptly addressed with aggression. As long as the adult dogs are well socialized and stable their reactions are usually appropriate and will not be overly aggressive, but just enough to let the younger dog know quite clearly that he has overstepped.

The younger dog normally backs down quickly, as he was simply testing the limits of acceptable behavior, just as adolescent humans do.

SIGNS OF STATUS

When two dogs meet the first thing they do is signal their status in relation to each other. They circle and sniff the other dog, gathering information through their noses and the giving and receiving of signals that determine if the stranger is male or female, friendly or hostile. The submissive dog in that interaction may look away or roll over, his ears may be back, and his tail down. The more dominant dog's ears will usually be erect, depending on breed; his tail may be up; he may loom over or mount the other dog; or he may rest his paw on the other dog's back.

BEHAVIOR PROBLEM: AGGRESSION

UNDERSTAND THE MESSAGE

WHAT YOUR DOG DOES

He may show his teeth, snarl, growl, nip, snap, bite, or lunge.

WHAT YOUR DOG MEANS

"I feel threatened."

WHAT YOU SHOULD NOTICE

Certain stimuli have motivated aggressive behavior in your canine.

Aggressive behavior can take many forms, from a dog's growl at not getting his way to a threatening lunge at a person or animal. Whatever the level of severity, it should be dealt with immediately.

commands and misbehave then he is the leader, not you; he will challenge your authority, and you won't be able to control his behavior around other animals. Dogs that recognize their owner as leader—the ones who are made to understand through rewards-based training what behavior is appropriate—are generally happy dogs and good family members.

Left unchecked, the first signs of aggression can quickly develop into advanced behavior problems. To prevent this, make sure your dog knows you are the leader from day one, not him. Training classes are also beneficial, but if your dog is already acting aggressively then more serious and immediate help is needed: visit your veterinarian to check for medical causes that might motivate the behavior; enlist an experienced behavior specialist, one that does not use punishment or excessive force as motivators, to work with your dog; understand the reasons behind aggression so you can manage situations where the behavior may be triggered.

UNDERSTAND AGGRESSION

A dog's people family may try to get him to sleep on the floor instead of the bed. Other canines may make direct eye contact. To the dog that sees himself as leader of the pack these actions may be interpreted as a social challenge, which can lead to the dog trying to prove his alpha status through aggression. Your dog's pack is made up of his people family and the canines he encounters. Hierarchy within the pack is communicated through body language and established through social challenges. If you allow your dog to ignore your

Fearful or defensive aggression occurs when the dog believes he is in physical danger. Perhaps because of past experiences or a lack of socialization he may see other dogs or a raised hand as a threat, whether they are or not. Protective aggression is motivated by a desire to keep his pack—including his people family and other animals—safe. Territorial aggression is triggered by a threat to what the dog perceives as his territory: his home and possibly the area surrounding it. Possessive aggression may result when the dog fears something that he views as his—toys, food, or sleeping area—may be taken from him. Redirected aggression is behavior that is directed not at the person or animal the dog fears, but to someone else because of proximity or opportunity. Movement—a squirrel or cat that is on the move, a jogger, bicycle, or car, for example—usually triggers predatory aggression.

Dog Fact

In multiple-dog households, the most common reason for fighting between dogs is a power struggle to establish who the alpha dog, or leader, is.

BEHIND THE SIGNS

Dog Fact

Well-socialized dogs tend to be friendlier and less fearful of the kinds of people and animals they were socialized to.

Let Sleeping Dogs Lie

Most of us know that dogs don't usually like to be interrupted while eating, and the same goes for when they are sleeping. If you suddenly wake them, even docile dogs may be frightened or angry, just as you might be if the situation were reversed. If you need to wake your dog, call him from a distance, giving him time to become oriented.

CAUSE AND EFFECT

Fearful pups are more likely to develop aggressive behavior, especially in stressful situations, while a dog that has been exposed to different sights, sounds, and a variety of experiences, people, and animals is generally a well-adjusted dog. He has been pleasantly familiarized with new experiences, and knows he has nothing to fear. This process is known as socialization and reputable breeders will start it at three weeks, just as the pup's senses awaken. The foundation of good behavior is laid during the impressionable weeks when the pup is three to 14 weeks old. However, socialization doesn't end at puppyhood. The process should continue after this period and throughout a dog's life.

During adolescence, your pup may start barking at people and become more protective and territorial. Continued training, consistently letting your dog know you are the leader, and regular socialization are necessary. Exposure to a variety of people—through classes, daily playtime at the park, and regular walks—and different experiences, such as riding in cars and buses, are key to reinforcing social skills and having a well-balanced and agreeable dog.

Older dogs may sometimes exhibit aggressive behavior even if they have never shown it before. There may be a variety of causes for this behavior, and the first step is to visit your veterinarian, as the behavior may be motivated by pain—arthritis, for example. If your dog can't move as quickly as he used to from possible threats, he may growl or bark instead. Senior dogs may also experience vision and hearing loss—two senses that they have depended on—and this can lead to fear that may motivate aggression. They may also be very set in their ways, so change, in the form of a move or a new addition to the family, may upset them and cause them to act out.

WHAT NOT TO DO

Punishment, of course, is never the answer. It communicates to the fearful dog that they were right to be fearful, tells the defensive dog that there is indeed a threat, and it can encourage the alpha dog to escalate his aggressiveness to prove his dominance. Instead, concentrate on rewarding good behavior so your dog understands that it is the behavior that gets him positive reinforcement and your attention.

Canine behavior specialists can work wonders with aggressive dogs but only if you enlist the right one. Do your homework; get recommendations from other dog owners and your veterinarian. Physical punishment is not the way that reputable specialists work. Besides being cruel, those methods can aggravate the existing behavior. Your dog, and every dog, deserves better.

Genetics, hormones, and environment all factor into aggressive behavior and dogs that have been cruelly treated or are spoiled are also at risk. Some dogs need very little motivation to react aggressively, while others have a higher threshold. Limit opportunities for the problem behavior by understanding what your dog's personal triggers are and avoiding those situations to keep your dog and others safe. See your veterinarian and enlist a reputable behavior specialist. After all, you are your canine's caregiver, and your dog is family.

Dog Fact

Aggression directed at the people a dog shares his home with suggests a lack of leadership in his owners.

BEHAVIOR PROBLEM: CHEWING

HOW TO TRANSLATE A GNAWING PROBLEM

Dogs are intelligent, social animals who need the stimulation of activity and companionship. Without it, the natural canine behavior of chewing can become destructive. If this is the case, a look at your dog's motivation can explain why he's behaving as he is, and what you can do about it.

THE WHYS AND HOWS

Puppies explore the world using their mouths. Most dog owners have experienced this—perhaps it was their shoes in tatters or couch cushions ruined. Dogs chew things—it is simply part of canine behavior—but accepting this doesn't mean accepting chewed table legs. Instead, ask yourself the following questions:

Is your dog teething?

The timing for this varies from dog to dog, but it is usually at about four months of age. During this time those sharp puppy teeth are shed and replaced by permanent adult teeth. Signs that may indicate teething include drooling, irritability, and changes in appetite, and your pup may mouth anything available to relieve his discomfort. Try soaking one of his stuffed or rope chew toys in water and then freezing it. Chewing on the frozen toy can help numb teething pain, and prevent your pup from chewing on things he shouldn't.

Is your dog bored or lonely?

If so, his behavior may be the only way for him to release energy or relieve anxiety. Your dog needs regular exercise, mental stimulation, and companionship. You can't always be with him, but don't leave him too long without first giving him the physical and mental exercise he needs, appropriate to breed. Ensure he has daily walks, training sessions to provide mental stimulation, time with you, and toys that will engage him when you are out.

Have there been changes in your household?

If you have recently moved, have significantly changed your work routine, or have brought a new baby or a pet home, your dog may be unsettled and anxious, causing him to chew for relief. Spend time with your dog and set a routine that will help him feel more secure.

Where do puppy teeth go when they fall out? It is quite normal for pups to chew and swallow the puppy teeth they shed, leaving no trace.

Does he have his own chew toys?

If he is busy chewing on his own toys, he will be less tempted by yours and whatever else he can find. The toy should be the right size for your dog—not small enough for him to swallow and not too large that it makes getting his mouth around it difficult. Balls, rope toys, hollow toys that can be filled with treats, and toys that make noises are often popular. Rotate the toys to keep them interesting.

 ## Dog Fact

Toys specially formulated for mental stimulation can keep your dog happily busy for hours. One example is "food-for-work" toys that can be filled with bite-sized dry dog food. To get at the food, your dog has to puzzle it out, or release it by rolling the toy around with nose or paw.

Home Alone

A dog crate can be useful for short periods of time as it keeps your dog away from your valuables. Crates, like baby cribs, are safety places. Most dogs enjoy time in their "den" or crate provided they have had the opportunity to become accustomed to it, are exercised before crate time, and have toys to keep boredom at bay when they are done resting and want to play. Dog crates should not be used for long periods; if you are out all day, you may want to use a baby gate to restrict your dog to a larger area.

DOS AND DON'TS

DO dog-proof your home. Place cleaning supplies and anything that could harm your dog out of reach.

DON'T leave electrical cords and cables exposed. These can be very appealing to canines, and very dangerous, so keep them tucked away.

DO ensure your garbage receptacle has a tight-fitting lid. The potential mess can be frustrating, but more importantly the garbage may contain choking hazards or food that could make your dog ill.

DON'T encourage your dog to play tug of war with a towel or T-shirt, or give him an old shoe to play with. He won't understand the difference between these items and the clean laundry or new shoes in your closet. Choose toys for him that do not look like household items and use only these toys when playing with him.

DON'T chase your dog if he runs off with an item he shouldn't. Being chased is fun and will only encourage his behavior. Instead, offer your dog a treat or call him to you.

DO train your dog to release objects. Offer him a treat in exchange for the item in his mouth, say "give" as he releases it and praise him. Do this consistently until he understands the command, at which time treats will not be necessary for each correct response, although praise should always be given.

Dog Fact

The teething stage is usually from about four months to the age of ten months, although it varies from dog to dog. Pups escalate chewing behavior during this time, as mouthing and chewing objects can relieve tender gums.

Not Guilty

If you come home to a canine-created mess, it is no use punishing your dog. He won't make the connection between his behavior and the punishment (after all, he may have chewed up your shoes an hour ago). He'll just understand that you are angry, which can cause him to fear you and your unpredictable (to him at least) moods. But he looks guilty, you say? He is not making eye contact, is submissively crouched down or crawling, or he ran away and hid when you came into the room? He is just reacting to your body language and tone of voice. It is not about the chewed shoes at all.

BEHAVIOR PROBLEM: DIGGING

A GUIDE TO UNDERSTANDING WHY DOGS DIG

Dogs dig. It's an instinctual activity, passed down from their wolf ancestors. Some dogs dig for fun, or because they have lots of energy and a need to explore their world, and some dogs dig more than others. Terriers, for instance, were bred for that purpose. Some dogs dig in an attempt to get themselves out of a frightening situation, like a thunderstorm, or because they are bored. Digging is part of a dog's DNA, but if the behavior becomes destructive, look to the cause. It will dictate your response and preventative measures and lead to better communication with your canine.

Is your dog digging for comfort or protection?

Dogs don't sweat as effectively as humans, so they don't cool off as efficiently. If your dog tends to dig in shady areas it may be because a hole dug in cool soil provides relief from the heat. Digging a hollow can also provide shelter from cold or wind, or it may simply be a den-like nesting spot for your dog.

Where and when is your dog digging?

If it is at your property fence and only happens when he is left alone he may be digging in an attempt to get to you. This may be a sign he is suffering from separation anxiety; he may see a dog or children on the other side of the fence as potential playmates; or he may instinctively feel the need to roam and explore.

Is your dog bored?

If he isn't getting the physical and mental stimulation he needs he may be digging to release energy that would have been better used in walks, training sessions, and appropriate play.

Does he hear or smell something beneath the surface?

Dogs have acute hearing and a keen sense of smell and some breeds, like Dachshunds, were bred specifically to burrow underground for prey. Dogs may dig out of curiosity about the source of an underground smell, or because their hunting drive instinctively goes after whatever it is they smell or see moving under the earth.

A Tired Dog Is a Good Dog

Playtime in the yard is not enough; dogs need daily walks and mental stimulation through games, toys, and training sessions. You could also arrange for supervised play dates with compatible dogs. The dogs involved should have a play style—chasing or wrestling, for example—similar to your dog. A pleasantly tired dog is a good dog, with less energy to be destructive.

YOUR RESPONSE

Like most forms of unwanted behaviors, it is easier to prevent destructive digging than to correct it. Make sure that your dog is getting daily exercise suitable to his breed. If there is one particular spot your dog likes to dig up, try changing its surface by adding stones. If it is prey such as underground moles or rodents that is the trigger, do your best to get rid of them, or keep your dog away from that area. If your dog is digging to find a cool spot, try providing him with a small children's pool or a shelter in a shaded area, and make sure he always has access to drinking water. Next, accept that dogs will dig but this behavior need not be destructive. Provide an area where it is okay for your dog to dig. This may be a child-sized sandbox or part of your lawn that is fenced below the surface area, but wherever it is ensure there is shade for hot days.

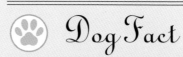

Dog Fact

If your dog sees you gardening, he may want to join in on the fun. He doesn't distinguish the difference between your actions and his; he just knows that digging in the ground is something you both enjoy, so you may want to keep him out of the yard during planting.

To encourage your dog to dig only in that area, bury some of his favorite treats and chew toys there, praising him when he finds them. Supervise your dog and lead him back to the designated spot if he wanders off to start digging in your flowerbed. Eventually he will understand, and if the designated area is fenced it makes your job even easier. To prevent boredom, rotate the treats and toys you bury. Freshly tilled soil is especially attractive to many canine diggers—as gardeners who are also dog owners know so well—so turn the earth over occasionally, adding fresh dirt. If your dog doesn't respond to his designated area then dive right in with your hands, digging for his treats to show him what to do. Let him know that in that space—but only there—digging is encouraged.

 Dog Fact

Non-neutered dogs may feel a powerful urge to roam, which they facilitate by digging a way out of the yard. If you are not planning to breed your dog then neutering is not only a responsible act, it can help save your yard from destructive digging.

INHERITED FROM WOLVES, ENCOURAGED BY PEOPLE

A look at our dog's ancestors shows just how integral digging is to dogs. Wolves dig to bury food in order to keep it safe from others and reclaim it later when they are hungry again. They dig dens to raise their pups, and to shelter from the weather. They dig up roots to supplement their food and are excellent below-ground hunters. They are, at heart, diggers, just as their descendants will be. Does your dog bury his toys and treats in the yard, or behind cushions in your home? This hoarding is also part of the digging ritual, meant to keep what your dog values safe from others until he needs it, just as wolves do with their food. Canines use their nose to bury things, for example when they nudge leaves along to cover a bone or act to "hide" the remains of their dinner by pushing their food bowl around with their nose. The instinct to bury extra food is there, even when there is nothing to hide it with. Does your dog dig at his bed, before lying down? It's another example of inherited behavior: he's doing as his ancestors did in the wild, digging a "hole" to shelter in.

Although our canines inherited this instinct to dig, we can't lay all responsibility at the wolf's den. People recognized that digging behavior could be beneficial at getting rid of vermin on farms, and selectively bred to encourage the prey drive. Terriers are an example, and their name reflects this; it comes from the Latin word for "earth," *terra*. Dogs dig with their front teeth, throwing soil under and behind, but certain Terriers have another trait—also encouraged through breeding—which makes them even better at digging: turned-out feet. This allows them to shovel dirt to the side instead of just back, where the growing mound of dirt could push them forward into the hole. Dogs may no longer need to hoard food or hunt vermin, so why is the behavior still so prevalent? Instincts passed down from wolves and complemented with selective breeding mean that old habits die hard, and digging is one of the many behaviors that make a dog the way he is.

THE EYE OF THE BEHOLDER

What seems destructive to you may just seem like fun to your dog. He doesn't know what he is doing is wrong unless he is taught, and he is not doing it to be spiteful—it simply relieves his pent-up energy, boredom, instinctual drive, or anxiety. But where dogs learn to dig, their activity and mental stimulation, and the quality of time they have with their owners will distinguish healthy canine activity from destructive behavior. It's really up to you.

BEHIND THE SIGNS

Dog Fact

You can't always control your dog's natural tendencies, but you can change your dog's environment and that can turn problem behavior into healthy activity.

Why Is My Dog Hoarding His Treats?

It is not because he doesn't trust you to make sure he's fed; it is simply a natural instinct to hoard, and part of the digging instinct to hide food for later. Many species share this instinct: mountain lions hide carcasses under leaves, squirrels hide nuts in soil, and the list could go on. Your domesticated dog is lucky enough not to worry about where his next meal is coming from, but the instinct to hoard remains, and some canines exhibit this behavior more than others.

BEHAVIOR PROBLEMS: INAPPROPRIATE

LEARNED BEHAVIORS WE TEACH OUR DOGS

WHAT YOUR DOG DOES

Jumps up at people by standing on his rear legs with his paws on the person's chest.

WHAT IT MEANS

An instinctive action acquired from their ancestors, it can show either submission or dominance, depending on the breed and age of the dog.

WHAT YOU SHOULD DO

Discourage the behavior from the start, either by closing off the space into which your dog can jump or by refusing to reward his behavior with attention.

I **t can be instinctive behavior, passed down from a dog's wolf ancestors, to solicit food or to offer a greeting. Licking another's lips is also used as a submissive gesture, but to get to the lips of someone taller our dogs need to jump up first. In older dogs, this behavior is often a display of rank. In canine-to-canine communication, one dog will loom over another and place his paws on that dog to show dominance.**

With the same intention our dogs will jump up on us and place their paws on our chest. Regardless of the intent behind your dog's actions, it has become a learned behavior—it got results so it was repeated.

What may be cute behavior when the dog is a puppy is less so as they reach their adult height and weight. Discourage jumping-up behavior from the start. A common deterrent is the body block; when your dog starts to jump up on you, turn sideways and lean over into the dog's space, so that he can't complete the jump or get his paws near your chest. Occasionally, you won't be fast enough to stop your dog so when this happens the best response is to ignore him. Look at the ceiling and do not speak to him until his legs are all on the ground again. You can also try walking forward as your dog starts to jump, so that he won't be able to balance on you and will be forced to put his front legs down. Whichever method works best for your dog, follow it up with the sit command and praise him when he responds correctly. Your goal is to prevent a successful jump and communicate to your dog that good things happen when he keeps four legs on the ground. With consistency, this behavior is relatively easy to overcome.

To prevent your dog from jumping up on guests to your home you can employ the sit-stay command, using it when the doorbell rings. Or you can hide a favorite chew toy near the door and distract your dog with that when guests arrive. Praise good behavior and ignore problem behavior.

From Wolf Cub to Canine Pup

Hungry wolf cubs jump up at their mother to greet her and to lick her lips, requesting with that action that she regurgitate her half-digested food so they can feed. Although our pups may not be looking for food when they jump up on us, the instinctive greeting behavior is still there.

WHAT YOUR DOG DOES
Begs for food from the table.

WHAT IT MEANS
The dog has been taught that begging for food from the table works. Pawing at food, whining, or barking with eyes focused on the food, or simply sitting beside the table and staring up at the food entreatingly are all learned behaviors and they do not mean that your dog is hungry.

WHAT YOU SHOULD DO
Never feed your dog from the table and make sure no one else does. Teach your dog that he will not be rewarded for begging and stand by your decision. The behavior can be annoying enough that you may want to give in—don't. Remind yourself that eating table scraps can lead to weight gain, and is a leading cause of canine digestive problems. Understand that our dogs learn what we teach, and if begging is rewarded they have just had a training session.

It's easy to notice inappropriate behavior, but good behavior doesn't always get a reaction, and it should. Look for good behavior and reward it, and ignore the rest. Not only will your dog learn that good behavior gets results, the positive reinforcement will increase your bond.

Apply this approach at the dinner table. The food we eat isn't always bad for our dogs; it's the manner they get it, by begging, that is the problem. Feeding your dogs greens or other healthy alternatives to complement his regular food can be good for him and can be offered as a reward to good behavior. Take care, however, to monitor the type of food you give him and limit those that are fatty, spicy, or very rich. Learn which foods are a danger to canines, such as chocolate, grapes, raisins, and onions.

Remember that inappropriate behavior has been learned. We have communicated that it is okay, either by not correcting the behavior or rewarding it. Instead, we need to provide a reason for good behavior, and no excuse for bad behavior.

TABLE SCRAPS AREN'T TREATS

Why begging behavior should never be rewarded:

- It can lead to problem eaters, who refuse dog food in favor of our food.
- Dogs who develop a taste for our food are more likely to steal food from the counter, or ransack the garbage bin for leftovers.
- It can lead to unhealthy weight gain and obesity, which leads to health problems.
- Dogs who are fed the occasional scrap lean that persistence pays off and will escalate the behavior.

- Much of the food we eat is too rich for our dogs and can lead to digestive problems.
- Table scraps don't provide the nutrition a canine needs.
- Bones can lodge in a dog's throat.
- Treats lose their effectiveness; why should your dog exhibit good behavior for treats when he can beg for food instead?
- Dogs are smart. Soon their begging won't be limited to the table, but will include when you open the fridge door and when you are cooking.

CANINE FAQS

A GUIDE TO UNDERSTANDING COMMON QUESTIONS

WHAT YOUR DOG DOES
Rapid, shallow breathing, with his mouth open and tongue protruding.

WHAT IT MEANS
Your dog is overheated and is regulating his body temperature by panting.

WHAT YOU SHOULD DO
Determine if his panting is normal or not. To do that, first understand why dogs pant and what could indicate a health problem.

People sweat when they're hot and dogs do too. For dogs, however, sweating isn't as effective a cooling method as respiration. Dogs have sweat glands in their ear canals and on the pads of their feet, but not in their skin, as we do, so panting is how they regulate their body temperature.

The more rapidly they pant, the more excess heat they release. Overweight dogs are more prone to panting because they overheat more quickly. Excessive panting can be worrying in short-faced breeds like the Pekingese, Pugs, or Boxers; their skull formation affects air passage, so they breathe differently than other breeds and this makes their panting less effective. Cooling is more difficult for them to achieve so they work harder by panting heavily. The best defense is to prevent dogs from overheating in the first place. Make sure they always have a shaded area outside with lots of drinking water, and keep them inside with air conditioning when necessary. There will be times when your dog will overheat, despite your efforts. Know that although your dog may look and sound uncomfortable he generally isn't. His internal body temperature radar has simply kicked in and, just as people produce sweat, dogs pant.

Some dogs pant when they are excited or fearful, in which case remove the cause and the panting should subside. Older dogs may also pant more as they age. How do you know when the panting may indicate a health problem? Familiarize yourself with what is normal panting for your dog and look for key indicators if the panting seems atypical: there is no trigger, such as heat, exercise, or overstimulation; it is more labored than is usual in that situation; or the frequency has increased.

BEHIND THE SIGNS

Feeling Blue

Excessive and unexplained panting may be a message that your dog needs medical attention. Check the color of your dog's gums; some dogs have naturally pigmented gums that are dark in color, but if this isn't the case in your dog then a bluish tinge can indicate respiratory distress, which can cause panting.

WHAT YOUR DOG DOES
Runs in circles, trying to catch his tail.

WHAT IT MEANS
Often nothing more than a playful game puppies play at a young age, although if it occurs regularly in older dogs, it may indicate a problem.

WHAT YOU SHOULD DO
If you suspect that the behavior is indicative of unrest, a trip to the vet might help identify an underlying health issue.

"*C*hasing your tail" is a saying used to describe a pointless, repetitive activity, but when your dog does it there may be a point. The message is in the frequency. Puppies often go through a tail-chasing phase, usually around the time they realize they have one. It is their kind of high-energy play, and they generally grow out of this phase, unless it becomes self-rewarding because of attention received, which leads to repeat performances. Other dogs may chase their tails in play occasionally and the message may be one of boredom and is a sign they need more exercise and mental stimulation. But if the behavior becomes common and intense it can communicate a problem.

MEDICAL COMPLAINT

If it is a recent and repetitive behavior there may be something bothering your dog in his tail region; this could be fleas, an anal gland problem, an injury, or another medical cause. If his behavior is frequent and so focused that you have difficulty distracting him, it could be a compulsive behavior. Breeds can carry the tail-chasing gene; in some dogs it is latent all their life, while others may not exhibit the behavior until a combination of genetics and environmental stress set it off. It could be puberty coupled with stress, and the stress may be something easy to pinpoint, like the owner spending more time out of the home, or something more difficult to ascertain, like the sound of the dishwasher.

The cause may not be obvious, but if you note when and where the behavior occurs and look for patterns it can help you figure out the trigger. Once you know what sets your dog off you can avoid the cause, if possible, or enlist a behaviorist to help curb the excessive behavior. Playful tail chasing can seem endearing and entertaining, but it can lead to injury, and, if frequent and intense bouts occur, it can signal a warning that all is not well. Whatever the reason, a medical checkup to rule out health problems should be your first step in getting your dog to stop running in circles.

Excessive behavior usually has a trigger. The timing of your dog's actions and the situation in which it occurs can tell you what it is for him.

STORM-PHOBIC CANINES

Dogs smell, hear, and feel a thunderstorm differently than we do. Their keen noses smell the change in the air, their sensitive ears feel the change in atmospheric pressure, and their superior hearing gives them an early auditory warning of the storm to come. When it does arrive, they hear the same thunder we do, but—because of their ability to hear at a greater distance than humans—at a much great intensity. Dogs are also very good at picking up our signals, so if we are tense and fearful this communicates to them that they are right to be frightened. The best response is business as usual. A light and confident tone says that everything is all right much better than soothing words and actions that can reinforce fearful behavior or be interpreted as a reward that encourages it.

At the start of the storm, try to distract your dog with one of his favorite games or chew toys. It may help relax him and redirect his attention away from the storm before he gets too worked up. If your dog isn't interested then leave it. If you try to force the game it will only create more anxiety. He may try to escape the storm, causing destruction in the attempt and to release anxiety. If there is a place that your dog generally feels safer during storms—typically the bathtub, under your bed, his dog crate, or in a closet—encourage this and make the space comfortable for him, but make sure he is able to come and go. Feeling trapped will only escalate his fear.

Dogs may develop a fear of storms at any point in their lives, although it often occurs between the ages of two and four and escalates with age. They don't need a bad experience, such as being left outside in a storm, to become fearful. It may simply be a combination of how their senses interpret the change in weather though wind, rain, air, a darkening sky, lightning, and thunder. If you can make each storm a pleasant experience for your dog early in life it may help prevent this, as he will associate storms with games and time with you. If your dog is already fearful of storms then create a calming environment: speak in a happy, assertive tone; keep windows covered so he can't see the storm; and create a safe space for him, shielded from the sounds of the storm if possible. Homeopathic remedies given before the storm, if you know it's coming, or at the start may also help your dog stay calm, such as a few drops of peppermint oil placed on the pads of your dog's feet. In extreme cases of fear your veterinarian may be able to prescribe medication to calm your dog or a behavior therapist can help modify your dog's storm sensitivity.

BEHIND THE SIGNS

Dog Fact

Fear of thunderstorms can become a fear of loud noises in general, or anything associated with the storm.

What Your Dog's Fear May Look Like

In the midst of a large thunderstorm, your dog's body may tremble and his eyes may be dilated. He may search out a safe hiding spot or stay as close to you as possible. He may drool, pant, bark, and pace and may have housetraining accidents, as well as trying frantically to "escape," injuring himself in the process. Gauge your dog's needs with sensitivity; he may not desire your company while the storm is overhead, preferring instead to retreat to a favored hiding place. Help him to establish a discreet spot, in advance of the stormy season, where he can lie unnoticed and feel safe.

3

WHAT YOUR DOG DOES

Eats grass and sometimes vomits afterwards.

WHAT IT MEANS

Professional opinion is divided. There are a number of explanations that are commonly put forward, although all agree that eating grass does not harm dogs.

WHAT YOU SHOULD DO

Understand the possible causes and use contextual clues to help you identify why your dog may be doing it. Above all, remember that this is a natural behavior.

*T**his is one of the most common questions dog owners ask and the answer is: no one really knows. We know dogs are curious and that one of the ways they explore the world is through their mouths, especially as puppies.***

Their sense of smell is highly developed, their sense of taste less so. The grass may simply smell good to them and so they eat it. Dogs may also eat grass out of boredom that leads to foraging if they spend too long in the yard without companionship or stimulation. Some experts theorize that dogs purposefully induce vomiting when they are suffering from gastrointestinal troubles by eating grass. Others believe that the dogs aren't eating grass to self-medicate, but that they vomit after eating it because grass is fibrous and not easily digestible. Another explanation may be that grass compensates for a nutritional deficiency, while others believe it is a hereditary behavior passed down by wolves, who supplemented their diet with roots and grass.

There is no definitive answer as to why dogs eat grass; it could be any one of these reasons or none. What is known is that eating grass is generally not harmful, as long as the grass hasn't been chemically treated with pesticides or herbicides.

Sign of Sickness?

Some dogs vomit after eating grass and this is not usually a sign of anything serious. He may have eaten too quickly—a common reason dogs vomit in general—he may have eaten too much, or have trouble digesting it. As long as the vomiting does not persist and your dog is bright and alert then there should be no cause for concern. If the symptom persists, however, then medical opinion should be sought.

4

WHAT YOUR DOG DOES
Rolls on garbage or anything foul-smelling.

WHAT IT MEANS
The interpretations vary, but understand that your dog may find the most unlikely scents appealing.

WHAT YOU SHOULD DO
Prevention is key. Rather than punish your dog for tracking down the source of the bad odor, take care to dispose of anything that may end up smelling bad.

What seems unexplainable behavior to us may make perfect sense to our canines. Dogs experience the world primarily through scent, and what can smell horrible to us is often especially interesting to them.

It may also be worth telling others about. To a dog, rolling around on garbage, dung, or rotting animal matter may be a way of communicating what he has found. This theory looks to wolf behavior for an explanation because, as scavengers, rolling around on decaying matter could advertise a possible food source to the rest of their pack. Others speculate that the hunting instinct in dogs leads them to roll around on foul-smelling things in order to disguise their own scent and allow them to sneak up on prey, just as wolves did. Another possibility is that dogs are not trying to absorb the scent of what they are rolling on but are attempting to cover that scent with their own.

Experts disagree as to the message behind the behavior, which is why it remains such a common question. How best to deal with it is agreed upon however: prevention. Parasites from the decaying matter are a possibility, and although our canines aren't bothered by the smell, prevention is a lot more pleasant for the people who live with them.

Dog Fact

After being bathed, dogs may be more inclined to roll in garbage and organic matter. It can cover the scent of any perfume from the shampoo with something that smells a lot more interesting to them.

Separation Anxiety

Distress when left alone is what sets dogs with separation anxiety apart from other canines. Problem behavior can occur with either, but untrained, bored, or underexercised dogs may engage in problem behavior at any time, whereas dogs with separation anxiety only react like that when apart from their owners. These dogs may show anxiety when they recognize the signs you are about to leave and may try to go with you. While you are gone they may bark, howl, have housetraining accidents, chew the furniture, scratch at the door—all in an attempt to relieve their anxiety and be reunited with you. When you arrive home there will be a big welcome waiting, not only in the destruction your dog may have caused but also in his frantic greeting. Separation anxiety may stem from a lack of socialization, a fear of abandonment, a change in the household or the dog's environment, or the dog may be genetically predisposed to the condition. It is not a result of disobedience or malice. Your dog is not trying to get back at you for leaving him; he is simply expressing his anxiety in the only way he knows.

HEALTH 101

WHAT BEHAVIOR AND APPEARANCE CHANGES CAN TELL YOU

*C*hanges in your dog's health can be indicated in many ways: through body language and vocalization, and also through differences in his appearance and behavior that can signify all is not as it should be. Part of understanding the secret language of dogs is knowing the cues that signify all is not well, so that you can catch potential health problems early and work with your veterinarian to make your dog as comfortable and healthy as possible. Cues can be very clear, such as mobility issues, or less obvious, such as increased thirst. Look for changes that are out of character for your dog. Sudden lethargy or aggression, a coat that is no longer shiny, and displays of a new behavior, like excessive head shaking; there is a message behind all these signals, one that you may need your veterinarian to help translate. This chapter will look at some common health conditions and the behavior and appearance changes your dog may exhibit that provide an early warning. Many symptoms may be common to more than one condition; for example, itching and chewing of skin could indicate fleas or the more serious condition of skin cancer. It's best to note all of your dog's symptoms and consult your veterinarian for diagnosis and treatment.*

HYPOTHYROIDISM: Unexplained weight gain and skin and coat problems are the most typical symptoms. Many dogs also experience decreased energy. Hypothyroidism is a medical condition in which the dog's thyroid gland is not producing enough thyroid hormone, which regulates his metabolism. It tends to affect mid- to large-sized breeds between four to ten years old. It is easily diagnosed through veterinarian-administered blood tests, and most dogs with the condition respond very well to medication that treats the problem.

JOINT PROBLEMS: Swaying, staggering, or a rolled gait; difficulty in rising from a sit or going up and down stairs; swelling or obvious discomfort when attempting to lie down can indicate joint problems, such as arthritis. Hip dysplasia in canines causes deterioration and weakening of a dog's hips and the effects are varied—it can be mild or it can cause severe arthritis. It occurs in dogs who have an abnormal development of the hip joint resulting in the head of the femur not fitting properly into the hip socket. Genetics play a big part in determining whether or not your dog will develop the condition with certain breeds, like Rottweilers and German Shepherds, genetically predisposed to the disease.

EAR INFECTIONS: Redness and swelling of the ear, odor, and discharge are signs of an infection. These signs may be emphasized by your dog rubbing and scratching at his ear. Ear infections are not unusual, particularly in dogs that swim a lot or have long, drooping ears. They are caused by parasites, fungus, or bacteria. If your dog is engaging in new behavior, such as rubbing his ears along furniture or the floor, scratching at his ears, or shaking his head, this generally translates to an ear infection.

ELBOW CALLUSES: Dogs that suffer from calluses may show an increased or new sensitivity when

Older Dogs

As dogs age they are more likely to develop health problems, just as people do. Although this is expected, any changes should be carefully looked at, as they can tell you what your dog may be suffering from so you know best how to help him. For example, older dogs are often less mobile than they were. This could be due to arthritis, but it could also be due to vision or hearing loss—two very different conditions. Look at your dog's symptoms against all possible causes, working with your veterinarian to resolve health issues.

WHAT THE SKIN AND COAT CAN TELL YOU

The condition of your dog's coat will tell you a lot about the state of his health. If it is dull, brittle, and listless, it may signal that he is not getting the necessary vitamins or nutrients. Excessive shedding can also communicate a problem. Dogs shed but if your dog is shedding more than he normally would and it is not seasonal or age-related then it may signal a coat or skin problem due to allergies, parasites, infections, or hormonal disturbances. Signs to watch for include scaly areas on the skin, red patches or bumps, and increased skin pigmentation, and your dog may scratch or chew on his skin for relief. Feed your dog nutritionally balanced food appropriate to his age and breed, groom him regularly, and watch for any signs that may signal a health-related problem.

their legs are groomed, or when they sit or rise. The condition is common to medium or large breeds, and results from laying on hard surfaces. To prevent this, ensure there is soft bedding and a carpet or blanket in the areas of your home in which your dog rests.

PARVOVIRUS: The symptoms included decreased food and water intake, severe vomiting, and diarrhea. Dogs of all ages and breeds can be affected if they come into contact with infected feces, although a regular vaccination schedule can protect your dog. If your dog's symptoms match those of parvovirus see your veterinarian immediately, especially if your dog has been in a commercial kennel recently.

SKIN CANCER: This is the most common type of cancer found in dogs, most usually in dogs aged six to 14 years old. Symptoms are similar to those that a dog with irritated skin experiences and may include discomfort and itchiness, bald patches, redness, scaly skin, and bumps under the skin. Look out for your dog itching more than usual, chewing and biting on his skin, or bumps on his skin that were not there previously. Causes are unknown, although it is thought that some breeds may be more susceptible.

DIABETES: If your dog is suddenly thirstier, urinating more often, losing weight, and has less energy than usual, these cues may indicate diabetes. It can affect any dog, although female dogs are twice as likely to be affected. Juvenile diabetes typically affects dogs younger than one year, while diabetes mellitus most often affects dogs aged seven to nine years. Diabetes is one of the most common hormonal diseases in canines, and occurs when the body's ability to metabolize sugar is impaired.

PERIODONTITIS: A decreased appetite, accompanied by bleeding gums, bad breath, gum recession, and possibly mouth ulcers may signal

periodontitis. Eighty percent of dogs may suffer from this disease, caused when gum inflammation or infection is left untreated.

KENNEL COUGH: A distinctive, honk-like cough, sometimes followed by retching. Dogs of any age and breed may experience this, but younger dogs are usually more susceptible. It is highly contagious, and is often spread through dogs that have been housed in close contact with other dogs. Additional symptoms may include a loss in appetite and labored breathing, which can develop into pneumonia if not treated.

RESPIRATORY ISSUES: If your dog is coughing more, or is experiencing breathlessness or excessive panting, this can often indicate respiratory problems, of which there are a variety of types and causes.

Look at your dog's eyes, nose, mouth, and ears. All should be free of excessive discharge. Eyes should be clear and bright with no cloudiness. There should be no sign of crusting on the nose and pigmentation may be pink or black. Cold, wet noses have long been associated with health; a dry nose, however, doesn't necessarily mean a problem. Your dog's mouth should smell fresh and the gums should be uniformly pink or black. There should not be a buildup of tartar on the teeth and no missing or broken teeth. Ears should look and smell clean with no sign of ticks.

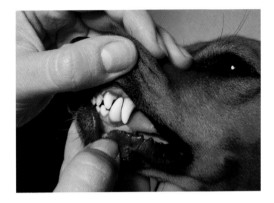

Now move on to your dog's coat, nails, spine, and abdomen; you can combine these checks with grooming. A healthy coat should be shiny and free of mats, dandruff, and fleas. The skin under his coat may be pink or black depending on his breed, and it should be smooth and clean, without any discoloring. Your dog's nails should be smooth, and either black or white. Next check your dog's spine and abdomen by gently feeling both areas; there should be no discomfort to your dog while doing this. During the first health check, you may find certain bumps and some of these are normal. It will be difficult at first to know which are okay and which aren't, but what you are really looking for are changes. If you do the check regularly you will become familiar with the normal state of your dog's body and therefore anything unusual much more quickly. Watch for fluctuations in your dog's weight; any significant change may require a visit to your veterinarian.

🐾 *Dog Fact*

Many dogs are very good at hiding pain or ill health, so extra attentiveness is important.

NOW HEAR THIS

Dogs with long ears that hang downward—like Irish Setters or Labrador Retrievers—are often more susceptible to ear problems, especially if they love to swim or they live in a humid environment. Head shaking or ear scratching can be a sign that your dog's ears need medical attention. Check for increased sensitivity to the touch, thick or waxy discharge, odor, swelling, and redness. Understand the message your dog's actions and health communicate, and see your veterinarian with any concerns.

SPEAK VOLUMES

HOW DOGS INTERPRET OUR ACTIONS

*D*ogs are experts at sending and receiving body language signals, whereas people are less so. There are certain cues we use, such as sitting forward to indicate interest or jutting our chins to show determination but, because our primary communication is spoken, we rely on words to get our message across. Not so with our dogs; they use vocalization as a secondary means of communication, relying on body language primarily. For people, it is the opposite—our words convey our message, although we may use body language, for example, motioning with our hands as we speak to provide emphasis.

You can talk to your dog as much as you like and he won't understand the words you use because his vocabulary is derived from physical cues that express intent and emotion. This canine skill often makes it seem like they understand our language, and to a certain extent they do. They may not understand from your words how bad the traffic was and how late it made you, but they understand through your body language that you are stressed. This communication goes a long way to solidifying the bond between humans and dogs, but it's also not without problems. Humans are primates, dogs are canids—two very different species with different social cues and body language. Sometimes the message we send is successfully interpreted, other times a very different translation is made, and at times we are unaware that we are sending a message, although our dog's powerful observation skills interpret it regardless. If we send too many unclear and conflicting messages we confuse our dogs, causing them anxiety that may prompt them to simply ignore us. Leaders should know how to communicate, and our ability or inability

 $\mathcal{D}og\,\mathcal{F}act$

Children have a hierarchical disadvantage given their tone of voice and height, which are typically interpreted by dogs as a sign that they are subordinate. Some dogs, if unsupervised, will take advantage of this and assert their dominance.

to do so speaks volumes to our dogs. Your dog gets to know you through your actions, so thinking about how best to communicate, and what messages you may be sending unintentionally, is important.

Quiet Authority

Hundreds of expert studies have looked at the dynamics of the dog litter and noted the calm authority of the mother dog. Although she may at times discipline her pups with a grasp around their muzzle, the primary method used to maintain alpha status is her attitude. It communicates responsible leadership and her pups respond to it by recognizing without question their role as lower in the hierarchy. This calm authority of the mother dog is a perfect example of leadership and one to be emulated so that we can more effectively "speak" to our dogs.

POSTURE

Since we stand taller than our four-legged canines we typically bend over to pat them, and this is meant as a friendly gesture. Unfortunately, our message can easily be interpreted as threatening and when we look at how dogs communicate with each other it is easy to understand why. Dogs establish hierarchy through non-verbal communication. A dominant dog may make himself as tall as possible when approaching another dog and may even rest his paw on the other dog's back upon reaching him. The second dog reacts by either accepting the dominant dog's action or by reacting aggressively. When we bend over the dog we are assuming the canine body language of dominance. The dog's response depends on his relationship with the person; he may react challengingly or submissively. Fearful dogs typically feel more comfortable with a person who is sitting down. They are less threatened and may approach a seated person but back away from someone who is standing. To approach a dog in a friendly manner, crouch so you are closer in height or, if standing, approach from the front or side with your hands low. This is more important with strange dogs, or on your first meeting with the dog who will be sharing your home. Once your dog becomes part of your family you become a member of his pack and, with proper leadership from you, the pack hierarchy is established with people as the pack leaders. The dog happily accepts this, and thus bending over the dog should no longer be interpreted as a challenge.

EYE CONTACT

Dogs usually avoid eye contact unless they mean to issue a challenge. If we make and hold eye contact with a dog the signal we send is one of confrontation, to which a dominant dog may react with growls and escalating aggression. A submissive dog may be fearful, and dogs that are very submissive may urinate as a placating gesture.

Experts disagree as to how this knowledge should affect our behavior. We want dogs to see us as the pack leader, so wouldn't looking them in the eye be a good thing if it communicates dominance? On the other hand, why create a situation that could trigger aggression? It makes more sense to communicate pack leadership with calm, consistent authority, rather than by threat. Our dogs should recognize us as pack leaders because we have proven they can trust our leadership rather than because they fear us. To this end, it is best to avoid looking directly into a dog's eyes and focus on the tip of his ear instead. You are making contact with your dog visually, but without issuing a threat.

OUR WORDS AND TONE OF VOICE

The well-known dog breeder and trainer Barbara Woodhouse recognized that dogs have an easier time learning words with a hard consonant sound and popularized the command words we use today, such as "sit," and "stop." Dogs can learn these words but they will not understand them if we string them together in a sentence. Although they can

Body position plays its part in how canines translate our messages. In people-to-people communication, leaning forward indicates interest, but dogs use that stance to repel others. It is an aggressive body position, meant to give warning.

learn to respond to command words, the cues we inadvertently use communicate much more than words. If you stand holding the door open and ask your dog "do you want to go out?" he doesn't understand the words yet the message behind the open door is very clear. The same commands used in the same way are the best ways of getting your message across, as dogs get confused if you say "sit" in one instance and "sit now" in another, and mean the same thing. The tone of your voice communicates more than the actual words you use. Try an experiment: say the same sentence to your dog using different tones. Your dog will usually mirror your tone of voice in his actions. For example, if you speak in a happy voice your dog will usually react playfully. To communicate authority, a low pitch is most effective, as a high-pitched voice is interpreted by canines as fearful, overexcited, or immature. Volume is important too; when you increase the volume your effectiveness as a leader is questioned, as leaders don't need to yell to communicate to their pack.

GREETINGS

As the owner of a dog, you're the one who must initiate the introduction of a new person to him. Tell the person to slowly extend the back of their hand and allow your dog to sniff it before they pat him, avoiding the top of the head and the shoulders. Children may be tempted to hug your dog and this can present a problem, depending on how the dog views their status. Your dog's mother corrected her pup's behavior and reinforced her leadership through contact with the nape of his neck. As a result dogs are sensitive to being touched in this area. Your dog may react aggressively if a small child he sees as subordinate tries to hug him around his neck, because they are inadvertently challenging his rank. The same action performed by someone he sees as dominant, as his mother was, will get no reaction. Walking straight up to a strange dog can also be interpreted as a threat. It is best to approach them from the side, just as canines typically greet each other, as it communicates to them that you mean no harm.

Dog Fact

Dogs look to our head and neck carriage for cues as to our status. People and canine body language is the same in this instance: a neck and head held high signifies confidence, while a bowed head communicates submissiveness.

Dogs are keen observers and, because they don't share our spoken language, we can't convince them of something with words if our body language, tone of voice, and energy don't match up. If you want to better communicate with your dog, keep this in mind at all times and project calm even when you're not feeling it. If you aren't calm, your message gets lost. Dogs simply can't hear it through all of the emotional static, or they will at least choose not to. Dogs disregard commands that are shouted or are overly emotional because this is a sign of instability to them, not a sign of leadership. If you want to speak volumes to your dog then don't increase your volume but project calm. Regardless of the words you use, your body language, tone of your voice, and the energy you project are what makes the greatest impression on your dog.

Keep Quiet

A mistake many first-time owners may make is to communicate with their dog as though they are human. The fluctuation in tone, mood, and the words used will not be easily interpreted and will more often than not lead to confusion. As well as limiting language to a series of set commands, the tone of voice should be uniform, with a light and friendly tone used to praise your dog and a harsher, lower tone employed to correct inappropriate behavior. You will quickly discover that consistent and controlled vocal communication will produce much better results.

LOST IN TRANSLATION

HOW DOGS INTERPRET OUR MIXED MESSAGES

We know the rules of human interaction, but we are considerably less clear on how to communicate with our canines. Dogs don't come with instructions attached and so our human-to-human communication patterns, as baffling as they are to our dogs, are what we fall back on. Word repetition, word inconsistency, using a questioning tone, and increasing frustration when we don't get the expected results are human habits that are not helpful to our dog's learning process—in fact, they slow learning down.

Dog Fact

The canine brain works differently from the human brain, so we can't assume our dogs are getting our message unless we communicate in a way our canine understands.

Effective communication makes for a stronger bond with your canine and is integral to successful obedience training, which results in a safer and happier dog. Avoid communication patterns that don't translate to dog language and you're on your way to an increased understanding of your canine, and they of you.

Consistency Is Key

Canine confusion is often caused by a person's words not matching their tone or expression. If you give the command "come" in a reproving tone and with a frown on your face, instead of the neutral and direct way you normally say it, your dog will not know what to do. Are you reproving him for something? Consistency is important in the command words you use and equally important in your tone of voice and expression when using them.

REPETITION

With another person we may repeat things when we don't get a response the first time. However, to a dog, this kind of repetition is simply confusing. If you issue a command and your dog doesn't respond there are two possibilities: your dog did not hear you, which is rare; or your dog did not understand, which is common. Repeating yourself to a dog that does not understand only confuses things further. It frustrates your dog and can make him anxious, because he doesn't know what is expected of him. Instead, be prepared to help your dog once you say a command. This may mean guiding him gently into position physically or luring him with a treat or toy, and then rewarding him. There is no need to get upset with your dog if he doesn't respond the way you wish; he is not trying to be difficult, you simply didn't communicate with your dog in a way he could understand.

INCONSISTENCY

While canines can be taught how to respond to certain words, they don't understand language as we do, so when we say "sit" in one instance and "sit down" in another, and mean the same thing, our dogs can become confused as to how they should respond. Consistency is key. Do you ever say "sit" and not follow through? Do you ever say "sit" and, if your dog lies down, you shrug and think, "close enough." If you do this you're not helping your dog; you're just confusing him further. Clear communication with consistently enforced commands should be your goal.

QUESTIONING

People often communicate with each other using a questioning tone, but this does not work when communicating with our canines, who understand tone better than words. "Max, sit?" sounds unsure, as if you—the pack leader—don't know what you want. A more effective approach is to state a command to your dog in the tone you might use if you were giving directions to someone. "Go down a block and turn right," would be an appropriate tone for "sit." That is calm, clear, confident, and perfect.

Dog Fact

Consistency in command words matter, just as your tone of voice does. Be calm and assertive with your dog for best results.

IMMEDIATE REWARD

Dogs live in the moment. When your dog responds as you wish, use positive reinforcement right away so that he has the chance to make the association between your command, his actions, and the praise. Even a delay of a few minutes between the dog's correct response and your praise can cause confusion. Positive reinforcement coupled with daily repetition will reinforce what your dog has learned and improve your communication.

FRUSTRATION

When our dogs fail to understand us we can become frustrated with them, although the fault is not theirs. Remind yourself that your dog speaks a different language and look for ways you can help make your words easier for him to understand. If your dog does not respond the way you hoped he would, ask yourself the following questions: "Was I clear?" "Have we practiced this command numerous times in a calm environment?" "Does he consistently respond in a calm environment?" "What was my tone?" Never scream at your dog or lose control. Your canine knows that the alpha dog doesn't have to raise their voice to get attention and if you scream at him he will question your position.

THE LEARNING CURVE

INTUITIVE AND TEACHABLE LEARNING

*O*ur dogs learn by trying out new behaviors and repeating those that get good results. Look at dogs who beg for table scraps. They edge as close to the table as possible, barking or whining while staring intently at the food. Finally someone gives in and the lesson learned is that begging works. Or you're reading the paper when the dog barks. You shush him, and return your attention to the paper. He barks again, you look up and shush him. The dog doesn't know what shush means, but he understands the power of barking: when he does it you pay attention to him, but when he is silent you turn your attention to something else. He has been rewarded for barking, and will remember and repeat that lesson. If you ignore unacceptable behavior, your dog will learn it's not effective.

Your dog is smart; he fussed when being brushed and his owner put away the comb, teaching him that fussing is an effective way out of having his rump brushed. Rewards equal repetition. The people, animals, experiences, and environments dogs are exposed to also teach them. The more they see and do, the less they fear. Bus rides or exuberant small children can be intimidating to a dog who has never experienced them, but if he has been exposed to those situations and his owner made sure that they were pleasant experiences, the dog learns he has nothing to fear. Since fear is so often expressed in aggression, socialization results in easy-going dogs with less cause to act out. The dog is mentally stimulated and curious—a perfect foundation for continued learning and training. The more you teach your dog about the world around him, the more comfortable he is in the world. Your dog is learning from you all the time. He learns through trial and error, your reaction to his behavior, and through what he is exposed to.

Back to School

Dog-training classes can help you understand how your dog learns, so that when class is over you can continue to use this information in the ongoing training of your dog. During classes your dog is exposed to people, other canines, and a different environment—all essential components to his development. Get recommendations and research different schools to find one where the trainers have positive training techniques and a sound knowledge of dog behavior.

You can help your dog gain smarts by working with him from an early age. It is important to expose him to the world slowly by introducing him to new people, animals, and environments, and making each new experience pleasant.

Cause and Effect

If your dog gets into the garbage cans and you try to teach him this is wrong by calling him to you and reprimanding him in an angry voice, he won't connect your anger with the strewn garbage. Dogs learn through immediate cause and effect, so he will interpret your anger as what happens when he responds to your call—not the lesson you want to teach your dog.

Dog Fact

It is important to remember that the opposite of reward is not punishment—it is no reward.

It is said there are as many training styles as there are trainers, but in actuality training styles generally fall into two schools: positive reinforcement or dominance training. Positive reinforcement training uses praise and rewards to shape and change a dog's behavior. Dominance training concentrates on pack behavior and uses forceful methods to train dogs as subordinate, such as the controversial alpha roll—flipping the dog onto his back and holding him in that position. The best training should be a combination of information: what you want your dog to do; the reason for your dog to do it; and when a reward will be given.

CLICKER TRAINING

Timing is all-important in training. When dogs are rewarded immediately upon responding to a command, they make the connection between the command, their action, and the reward. The faster the reward is given the easier it is for the dog to make the connection. Even a five-second delay is too long for a dog to connect the dots as by then he has already moved on. Clicker training solves this problem by using a small device to create a distinct metallic sound. First the dog is taught through repetition that when he hears the click he gets a reward. Once the dog associates the sound with the reward, the clicker is incorporated into training sessions and, for example, just as the dog's bottom makes contact with the ground in the sit position the clicker is used. The dog hears it and knows he will get a treat, and because of the timing he can connect the reward more easily to his actions.

Understanding pack behavior helps you understand your canine, but forceful and physical training is not necessary, and can be dangerous. Adherents to dominance training may defend their position as wanting their dog to respond to them rather than rewards. The reality is that rewards are only a method of helping your dog understand commands and what behavior you expect. Once your dog understands this, rewards are not necessary each time.

Food treats are not the only rewards that work either. They can be very effective since dogs are food-motivated, but many dogs will also respond well when the reward is a walk or game. We all work for rewards, whether it is employment that results in a paycheck or following the conventions of acceptable human behavior, which results in pleasant social experiences. Our dogs are no different. When we ask them to "sit" before placing their food bowl on the floor or reward them with a game of catch after a training session, they are "working" to fulfill their need for food, toys, and attention. Positive reinforcement training gets positive results.

Why Do Some Dogs Seem Smarter Than Others?

Just like people, each dog has his own personality and strengths, and each has the capacity to learn. Differences may be a result of genetics, breeding, temperament—some dogs are more stubborn than others—and socialization, which makes the dog more open to different experiences like training.

SIT, STAY, DOWN, COME

SPEAK THE LANGUAGE OF TRAINING

*D*ogs are not born knowing they shouldn't chew the furniture or jump up on people. Obedience training is necessary for a peaceful coexistence, and is a kindness to your dog. When he responds to the "stay" command while you wait to cross the street you are keeping him out of danger. Training teaches your dog acceptable behavior that makes him welcome when you take him out of the home; it teaches him a common language and strengthens the bond between you; and it builds your dog's confidence. A trained dog knows what behavior is expected of him, and this clear communication makes for a relaxed and happier dog, and a more enjoyable companion.

What behavior do you expect from your dog? Think about this before your first training session and share your expectations with everyone in your home. Consistency is key. If one person allows a behavior that you are discouraging then training won't work.

THE POWER OF POSITIVE REINFORCEMENT

There are many methods you can use to train your dog and entire books devoted to the subject, but it doesn't need to be complicated. The simple positive reinforcement techniques outlined in this chapter are proven methods for teaching your dog the basic obedience commands—sit, stay, down, and come. No special equipment or skills are needed, but patience is the dog owner's secret weapon. Don't try to rush your dog; all dogs learn at different rates, so go at your dog's pace. Training sessions that are short and frequent are proven to be more effective. Ideally no more than ten to 15 minutes per session, two times each day, and then informal practice throughout the day. Link obedience to things your dog enjoys. Next time your dog asks for something—anything—have him do something

Dog Fact

Behavior that can be endearing in a pup may be less so when he is fully grown and at his adult weight. Training is best started early, but it is never too late to begin.

for you first. If he scratches the door to go out, ask him to come to you, then let him out. If he drops his ball in your lap, tell him "down." Before you put your dog's food bowl on the floor ask him to sit, and once he does, put the bowl down and praise him. Be creative and have fun, but have your dog respond to you before you respond to him.

Teach your dog at times when he can learn. Just like school, you have to do homework before you can expect to do well on a test. Calling your dog when he's chasing a squirrel, saying "down" when he's jumping on guests, or asking him to stay when there is a ball being tossed in the next yard are all major tests. Homework, in the form of training sessions, is required to succeed.

Rewards

Pick one of your dog's favorite treats to use as a motivator during training, ensuring that it is small and quick to eat so you don't lose momentum during the session. Schedule training sessions so they don't fall just after your dog's mealtimes; he won't be as interested if he is full. As your dog becomes more responsive to the commands, food rewards will not be necessary each time and can be reduced. Praise, however, should always be given when he responds correctly. Make sure your dog gets the appropriate exercise so he can work off the additional treats he receives during training sessions.

"SIT" COMMAND

The "sit" command is the perfect starting point, as it is the most common command and it is a simple lesson for your dog to grasp.

- Stand in front of your dog and place a food treat in the center of your hand, letting your dog see it, and then close your hand around the treat.
- With your closed hand just above your dog's face, move it slowly toward the back of his head as you say "sit." As his head goes up and back to follow the treat he should sit automatically.
- Praise your dog and reward him with the treat while he is still in position—this is very important—so that he associates his response with the reward.
- Repeat this exercise daily until your dog sits immediately at the command.

Tip: In step 2, be careful to keep your hand just above your dog's head. If you raise your hand when moving it back your dog will likely jump for the treat, rather than sit.

 Dog Fact

Always end training on a positive note so that your dog looks forward to the next session. If he does not understand a command then go back to something he knows so that you can praise and reward him.

"STAY" COMMAND

This command teaches self-control and is really just a long sit, so it is easy to teach once the sit command has been mastered.

- Stand a few steps in front of your dog and give him the sit command.
- When your dog is in the sit position, say "stay," while putting the palm of your hand in front of his face.
- Take a step back, keeping your palm open and repeat the word "stay" a few times.
- Give your dog a treat and praise him if he maintains this position for a few minutes. It's very important that your dog gets his reward while he is in position. If you give it to him once he has moved he may think he received the reward for moving.
- Release your dog from this position with a clap and an enthusiastic "OK!"
- If your dog breaks the stay then calmly return him to the position he was in. Do not reward, and try again. Practice daily until your dog understands this command, at which point you can then teach him the advanced versions, which may take him longer to understand. This involves:

a) Distance—Stand a bit further back each time you give your dog the command, rewarding him and then releasing him when he responds correctly.

b) Duration—Stand close to your dog, increasing the time he remains in the stay position before rewarding and releasing him. Don't expect your dog to remain in this position for long periods of time, or if you leave the room.

Tip: Take the training slowly, and do not try to practice distance and duration at the same time. The further away you go, the less time your dog will remain in position, and the closer you are the longer he will hold the position. Be sure to use the release and keep your expectations realistic.

Dog Fact

Start training in a quiet environment, such as a room in your home. Gradually increase the difficulty as your dog progresses by introducing distractions and moving the training to your yard or a park. A trained dog responds to commands regardless of what is happening around him and this helps keep him safe.

"DOWN" COMMAND

When your dog successfully responds to the down command each time you will then be able to ask him to stay from this position. To teach the down command:

- Stand in front of your dog with a treat in your hand and ask him to sit.
- Place the hand holding the treat in front of your dog's nose and then slowly move your hand straight toward the floor while saying the word "down." Your dog should follow the treat and lie down.
- Praise him and give him the treat while he is in position and continue to practice daily until your dog lies down each time.

Tip: Be careful that you do not move the treat forward as you move it to the floor, as this may result in your dog standing up to get closer to the treat.

BEHIND THE SIGNS

Hands that Talk

Hand signals are the primary means of communicating commands to deaf dogs. The training methods and time involved are no different than teaching a hearing dog, as all dogs learn through repetition. Think about when two dogs meet; although they may bark or growl, their primary means of communication is through body language first and scent second. If your dog is hearing-impaired, his powers of observation have been put to great use in watching you and his world so there is no impediment to obedience training. You can still talk to your dog—it is simply that, instead of verbal commands reinforced by hand signals, your dog will rely solely on silent commands.

"COME" COMMAND

Teaching this command is not difficult, but it may take longer for your dog to understand the desired response, and some trainers believe that dogs younger than two years will not respond to this reliably each time.

- Give your dog either the "stay" or "down" command.
- Once he is in position, take a few steps back from your dog, say his name, and then say "come" invitingly. Alternatively, you can also try bending down with your arms extended and wide open while saying "come" in a happy voice.
- Praise him and give him a treat immediately when he comes to you, and continue to practice regularly.

Tip: Never use the "come" command and then reprimand your dog for something else or perform an action he dislikes, like cutting his toe nails. He will associate the command with the reprimand or action, and will be hesitant the next time he hears it.

Dog Fact

If you decide to send your dog to a training school, ask your vet and other dog owners for recommendations. Research the school and ask to sit in on a class so you can evaluate it. Reputable classes use positive training techniques only, the trainers are experienced and calm, they have control of the dogs, and there is a reasonable trainer-to-dog ratio.

TRAINING TIPS

Training should be fun.

Your dog will sense if you aren't enjoying it and he won't enjoy it either. He also won't look forward to the next session.

Short, frequent training sessions are best.

To keep your dog motivated, twice-daily sessions of no more than 15 minutes each are better than twice-weekly sessions of an hour. If the training session goes on for too long your dog will be frustrated and the learning process will go backward.

Don't rush your dog's training.

Make sure your dog understands and is comfortable with a command before moving to a more difficult command. If he doesn't respond to a command after repeated attempts don't reprimand him but also do not reward him. Go back to an earlier command that he understands, praising him for the correct response and building his confidence, and work up from there.

End on a positive note.

You want your dog to look forward to his training, so when the session is coming to a close give him a command you are sure he can perform and reward him when he completes the command.

Always remain calm.

If you yell at your dog he won't respect you because, as the leader of the "pack," you shouldn't have to raise your voice for attention.

Training should never involve punishment.
Don't acknowledge misbehavior by your dog with punishment. If you lose your temper and yell at your dog you may be reinforcing his behavior by giving him attention, even if it isn't positive. The chances are your dog isn't misbehaving at all—he just doesn't understand what is expected of him. With patience and consistency from you he will eventually understand what behavior is acceptable.

To motivate your dog, reward him.
Reward him with what will motivate him most, including praise and treats in each session. If the training session occurs just after your dog has eaten then a food reward may not motivate him as it would if it were used before a meal. If he has been alone most of the day and you have just returned home from work, the best reward may be petting and praise. Figure out what best motivates your dog for each training session.

BEHIND THE SIGNS

Job Done?

A trained dog is one that responds to "come" even when he was just about to introduce himself to another dog, interrupt a game of frisbee at the park, or run down the street after a cat. Many dogs respond to commands if they have nothing better to do, but an obedience-trained dog responds to commands even when there are distractions, and this is what keeps him out of harm's way.

SIGN LANGUAGE

Hand signals can complement your training, giving you a way to communicate with your dog in situations where he can't hear you but can see you. These signals are really just another form of "language" between you and your dog, one that comes easily to most dogs given their talent for observation from a distance. Training your dog to recognize hand signals is best started once your dog is already very responsive to voice commands. To begin, combine the familiar command word with the hand signal; your dog will soon learn to associate the signal with the command and—with practice—will respond to either the silent or verbal cue. Common signals for the four basic commands follow, but whatever signals you choose to use, the most important rule of training remains the same: consistency.

SIT: Start with your arm at your side and move your hand up until it is at your face level, palm open and facing your dog.

STAY: With your dog in the "sit" or "down" position, hold your hand in front of his face, palm open (in the stop sign hand signal).

DOWN: Use your outstretched arm to motion toward the floor with your hand open, palm down.

COME: With your arm outstretched, bring your hand across your body to the opposite shoulder (as if you were waving your dog over).

When your dog is first learning, reward every time he responds correctly.

This helps your dog understand what you expect from him. Once he understands the command, you should decrease the food rewards to every three or four times he performs correctly, to let him know he won't always be getting a treat when he responds to commands. As you decrease the treats, continue to praise your dog when he responds correctly.

Don't overpraise.

Rewards and praise are important tools to communicate to your dog that he has done something that pleased you. However, if you overpraise, he may be so distracted that he doesn't remember what it is he's being praised for. Dogs have very short attention spans. Praising your dog by petting him and saying "good dog" in a happy voice, and giving him a small treat are enough to reward him. Just like training, praise should be consistent in manner.

Timing is important.

In order for your dog to understand that he is being rewarded for his actions he should be rewarded immediately. If you reward him five minutes later he may enjoy the treat and praise, but he won't associate them with his training.

Be realistic.

If your dog is full of energy it will be difficult for him to concentrate on training commands that involve being still, such as "sit" or "down." Take him for a walk first and then begin the training session.

Commands should be short.

The longer and more complicated the command word is, the more trouble your dog will have recognizing it.

Dog Fact

If your dog is excited, he typically doesn't listen well. It has been found that, even in an excited state, a dog will more frequently respond to a hand signal than to a verbal cue.

FUN AND GAMES

MENTAL AND PHYSICAL STIMULATION THROUGH PLAY

*D*ogs love to play. It is integral to their development and keeps them mentally and physically stimulated, lessening the chance of boredom-related behavior problems. Games can be made more or less challenging, and can be adjusted to suit the activity level of your dog. There is a game for every dog and a variety of interactive games that you and your dog can play. Whatever works for you, it is a great way to enhance the bond between you and your canine companion.

LOW ACTIVITY LEVEL

Let's Dance

Say the word "dance" and then gently reach down for your dog's front legs and lift so he is standing on his hind legs. Praise him, continue for a few seconds, and then place his legs back on the ground. Repeat, until he understands the "dance" command, and then see if he is able to do it without your assistance. Your dog's size contributes to his ability, as smaller dogs have better balance and tend to be natural dancers.

Tip: If your dog likes to jump up on people, the "dance" command can be an effective distraction. When you see the telltale signs that he is about to jump up, ask him to dance instead, and praise him when he does.

The Nose Knows

Put a treat in one hand and close your fingers around it, without letting your dog see. Ask your dog to sit and with both hands closed invite your dog to pick a hand, giving him the stay command if he attempts to get closer. If—by paw, nose, or look—he focuses on one hand, open it and give him the treat if there. If he picked the empty hand then open your other hand to show him the treat, but don't give it to him. Move your hands behind your back so he can't see into which hand the treat goes. Then, holding your hands in front of your dog, start again, rewarding him when he picks the correct hand.

Agility

This is a team sport and the team is made up of two: you and your dog. It involves directing your dog through a sequence of obstacles such as hoops, tunnels, and seesaws, using only voice commands and hand signals. It can be done in competition, or purely for fun. Look for clubs or classes that are safety-conscious and use positive reinforcement techniques. The benefits are many: mental and physical stimulation, increased confidence, and intense bonding through the enhanced human–canine communication that you'll share with your dog.

Simon Says

Use all of the training commands your dog knows, saying "sit" in one instance and "down" in another. Switch up the order in which you give the commands and praise your dog immediately for each correct response. Close your eyes before giving some commands, or turn your back on your dog. This increases the challenge, as most dogs get distracted easily or are less motivated to respond when they are not looked at. The goal here is to reinforce obedience training in a fun way and to encourage your dog to focus on the voice command.

Basketball

Find a large container such as a cooking pot, laundry basket, or small garbage can, and weigh it down so it won't be easily knocked over. Give your dog a toy or ball that he can easily grasp by mouth and lead him to the container. Instruct him to drop the ball, praising him when he does. Repeat this action several times until he gets the hang of it.

Jumping Through Hoops

This is an impressive trick that is quite easy to teach your dog, and as the challenge is increased it can also help him work off excess energy. Wedge a plastic hula-hoop into a door frame, with the bottom of the hoop touching the floor. With your dog on one side of the hoop and you on the other, encourage him to come through the hoop using an upbeat voice. As soon as he does, praise him and give him a treat if you choose. Repeat the exercise until your dog comes through the hoop readily and then increase the challenge. Hold the hoop steady, slightly raised from the ground and encourage your dog to come through. Keep practicing, raising the hoop slightly each time.

SAFE TOYS

Choose toys that are appropriate for your dog's size and strength. Tennis balls work well for small- to medium-sized dogs, but could lodge in the throat of a larger breed. Remove any small or dangly pieces that come with toys as they are choking hazards, and pay attention to the condition of the toy. A rope or chew toy that has been much loved can disintegrate, making what was once a safe toy a choking danger. Choose bone toys that are safe to consume— there are a variety of brands available—or are made of durable rubber, and avoid bones that could splinter and lodge in your dog's throat.

Work-for-food toys like sustained release balls can keep dogs engaged and mentally stimulated as they puzzle out how to get to the treat. Avoid giving your dog household items like old shoes or socks as toys, as this teaches dogs that these items are okay to chew on and he won't be able to differentiate between the ones you gave him and the ones you wear. When playing retrieving games, stay away from sticks with sharp ends or that are splintered. Two or three toys at any one time are enough, and to keep your dog interested in them, replace with others periodically.

MEDIUM OR HIGH ACTIVITY LEVEL

Hide and Seek

People and dogs have been playing hide and seek in various forms for countless years, as it's an easy game to communicate and a proven dog-pleaser. When you are out of sight of your dog, use his name to call him to you. When he finds you, praise him in an excited manner. Give your dog the "stay" command, hide again, and then call him to you. As his skill improves, make your hiding spots more difficult to find, using his name to call him again if he seems to be getting distracted or bored with his search.

Fetch or Catch

Retrieving games are great for active dogs who need strenuous activity. Some dogs are natural retrievers, although all can learn. For less active dogs, keep the length of the game and retrieval distance short, stopping when you see they've had enough. Throw a ball or frisbee and tell your dog to "fetch" or "catch" and praise him when he retrieves the object. Some dogs will run back to you with it naturally; other dogs will have to be called so you can repeat the process, until they know to return to you.

Dog Fact

Just like people, dogs learn things through repetition. Keep practicing, until your dog understands the game.

 ## *Dog Fact*

You choose when to start the game, not your dog. It's your decision as alpha, and doing so reinforces your role in the hierarchy.

Safety First

Puppies should avoid high-impact activities until they are fully grown, when there is a reduced risk of damage to their developing bodies. They can then move on to high-energy activities. Dogs, like people, need to build up endurance in sport. All dogs should avoid strenuous activity in hot weather. Make sure they have lots of water and shade to cool off in, and watch for signs like panting and glassy eyes that can signal they are overheated.

Obstacle Course

Start out with an easy course, and as your dog's skill increases keep him interested by making the course more difficult. More challenging obstacle courses are a great way to practice the heel command amongst distractions. Set a group of chairs up inside or outside, wherever you have enough room. Space the chairs far enough apart that both you and your dog can maneuver between them easily. Lead your dog into the obstacle course with the word "heel" and weave in and out of the chairs, praising him for staying close. You may want to add obstacles to the course—a table or a bench, for example—to add interest and to teach your dog a new word. With the object between you and your dog, say "under" as soon as he moves beneath it and then praise him immediately when he reaches you. With lots of practice the word "under" can be added to the list of words your dog understands.

Soccer

Use a ball appropriate to the size of your dog, and one that he can't pick up with his teeth. Start by gently kicking the ball along the ground toward your dog, then give him a chance to get involved. It may take him a few tries to figure out he needs to use his nose or paws to move the ball forward, so praise him when he does. When he bats at the ball with his paws or nudges it with his nose hard enough to send it a small distance away this is your cue to get involved again. Kick it along the ground, moving closer to him, and then let him take over for bit. Make sure there is lots of give and take to keep him interested.

Puzzle Play

Put a few food treats and a chew toy or two into a large box. Fill the box with newspaper, hiding some of the treats inside balled paper. Seal the box according to your dog's skill—the first time you do this you may want to let him see you put the treats in the box and use a box without a lid—working up to a fully sealed and perhaps even tied box. Cut a few small holes around the box so your dog can smell the treats, and then let him at it. Puzzling out how to get at the treats can keep him busy for hours and, although you may have a bit of a mess to clean up afterwards, you'll also have a happy and mentally stimulated dog.

Find It!

This is a classic dog game, in which dogs use their sense of smell to locate treats or toys. If your dog is new to the game, make it easy for him at first. Give him the sit-stay command and let him see you put the treat behind the couch or door. Release him from the stay and say "find it," praising him when he does. Gradually increase the difficulty by giving him the stay command and then hide things in another room where he can't see you. Try the bathtub or under a towel on the floor as he gets better at the game. More interesting hiding places will make things harder to find, meaning a happy and engaged dog for longer periods of time. If he becomes frustrated and gives up, you may have increased the challenge too quickly, so start again using an easier hiding place.

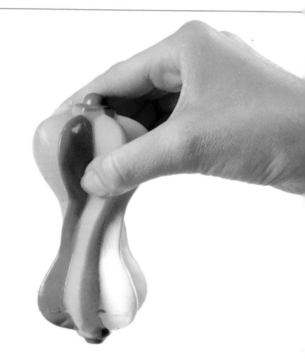

THE RIGHT GAME AT THE RIGHT TIME

Some dogs want nothing more than to play high-energy rounds of fetch, while others favor mentally stimulating games like hide and seek. Try to balance this out by playing games of both varieties and picking the game that best matches your dog's mood at that time. If he has been cooped up for a while, a high-energy game may be best; if he's just returned from the dog park or a long walk then choose a low-energy game.

THE ATHLETE: With lots of energy to burn, these dogs gravitate toward retriever games like fetch, catch, or flyball, and enjoy accompanying you when you rollerblade or run.

THE BRAIN: This dog gets bored easily and is engaged by games and toys that are mentally stimulating, like hide and seek or sustained release/puzzle toys.

THE COUCH POTATO: Low-energy dogs need exercise too, but during playtime may enjoy less active pursuits, like Simon Says.

AGES AND STAGES

PUPPYHOOD AND ADOLESCENCE

The first months of a pup's life are critical to his development. During this time, puppies learn from their mother and littermates the social cues and body language they will use for life. Playing with their littermates teaches appropriate behavior and submissive and dominant signaling. A pup that is separated too early from his mother and littermates has a more difficult time speaking canine, which affects their relationships with other dogs. Without an understanding of pack behavior or the signaling language that canines use, they are typically more fearful, which translates into aggression. Socialization during a pup's first three months is especially important. If he learns early on that people, animals, and everyday objects and experiences are not to be feared, he is more comfortable in the world and emotionally balanced, neither too submissive nor too dominant.

Although puppyhood plays a significant role in determining the type of dog the pup will grow into, even dogs who have not spent time with their littermates or been properly socialized can catch up. With your help they can learn the social skills necessary to be happy and contented dogs and good companions, as training and socialization should be practiced throughout a dog's life.

Adolescence is a time of change for your puppy. Your well-behaved puppy may be showing signs of aggression during this period and it's important to recognize and curb any aggressive behavior quickly. He's not a puppy anymore, but he isn't an

 Dog Fact

Puppyhood generally spans the first two years of a dog's life, although some breeds exhibit puppy behavior for longer or shorter periods.

adult yet either. He still has some growing up to do and he needs your help and training to develop into a well-adjusted adult dog. Watch for the signs of adolescent aggression and don't make excuses for your puppy's behavior. Excusing problem behavior because "he's usually so well behaved" is easy to do and understandable, as during this period your pup's behavior may seem very unlike him. Doing so, however, doesn't help your pup to grow into a well-mannered and even-keeled dog. Signs of aggression may be subtle but if not caught early your puppy's aggressive behavior can escalate and it's much easier to prevent problem behavior early on than retrain later. For example, your puppy jumps up on you in greeting, you give him the "sit" command but he instead leaves the room. You may rationalize that although he ignored your command his disobedience wasn't really important because the same end was achieved—he stopped jumping up on you. But in your pup's mind he has just won and he may push the boundaries a bit further the next time. Testing the boundaries is normal puppy behavior; many pups become possessive with their toys during this stage, growling if anyone goes near them. Or they become territorial, growling if anyone sits in the chair they have claimed as their own. Correcting your pup's behavior is your job as caregiver and pack leader, and will go a long way in enhancing your bond and relationship.

Dog Fact

From birth until at least eight weeks of age, your pup's mother is pivotal to him and influences how he will develop physically and emotionally. Pups feed off their mothers literally and figuratively: both food and the mother's emotional state—whether fearful or confident—are absorbed.

PUPPY DEVELOPMENT CHART

Neonatal Stage
Birth to Two Weeks

- Puppies are born with their sense of smell, touch, and taste but cannot see or hear.
- They are entirely dependent on their mothers. They cannot regulate their own body temperature or expel waste products without stimulation from their mother.

Transitional Stage
Two to Four Weeks

- The pup's eyes and auditory canals open, so he can communicate with his mother and littermates.
- Sight is still very limited until the fourth or fifth week.
- Pup becomes more mobile and vocal toward the end of this period. He can stand and begins to walk and bark.

Socialization Stage
Three to 12 Weeks

- Pups are highly impressionable and experiences are imprinted during this time, making it a crucial socialization period.
- At about the fourth week, a pup's senses are fully developed and he becomes more aware of his environment.
- He begins to carefully observe the people and canines around him, but is still most influenced by his littermates until week six.
- During this time he wrestles and play bites with his littermates, which helps him to begin to understand canine behavior and social skills, such as pack ranking.
- By approximately five weeks, pups have generally become more curious and socialization with people should be experienced.
- He will begin to recognize his name and respond to it.
- Weaning starts at approximately week seven or eight.
- Weeks seven to nine see improved coordination and full use of a pup's senses.
- Pups go through a fearful period, usually between weeks five to eight, and during this time they need careful handling and positive experiences with people, animals, and their surroundings.
- At nine to 12 weeks, the skills they have been developing through exploration and interactions with their littermates are more refined, and training can begin.

PUPPY DEVELOPMENT CHART

Ranking Stage
Three to Six Months

- Pups will typically play dominance games with their adopted family to test the boundaries and establish rank in their new people pack.
- They are more independent during this phase, a time that is commonly observed as being similar to the "terrible twos" in humans.
- Play biting should be discouraged and the pup's human family must consistently let the pup know they are the pack leaders.
- Teething starts during this period, which can lead to problem chewing behavior, so this is a crucial time in teaching appropriate chew behavior.
- Pups experience a second fearful period around month four, so ensuring pleasant socialization to people, animals, and new experiences is especially important.
- At approximately month six sexual maturity and adolescence is reached.

Adolescence Stage
Six to Eight Months

- The pup may exhibit scenting and marking behavior.
- Pups are often more aggressive during this period as they test boundaries, similar to the teen phase in humans. Behavior should be closely monitored and dominance discouraged.

AGES AND STAGES

THE OLDER DOG

*T*he newborn pup grows into an adolescent dog who matures into an adult dog, and continues to age until he reaches senior dog status. The stage at which this happens is dependent on the breed and their life expectancy. Smaller dogs generally live longest, with a life expectancy of 15 years or more, while giant breeds typically don't live as long. As your dog enters his senior years you will notice that his sleeping patterns change, his activity will decrease, he may have trouble moving around, and he may be less interested in the people and activity in the home.

BEHIND THE SIGNS

Your dog may begin to exhibit problem behaviors that are out of character. This does not mean he is experiencing senility and has forgotten his training. He may simply be unable to act differently because of age-related pain or the confusion and fear that accompanies decreasing senses, such as vision and hearing.

Decreased mobility may be due to a health condition such as arthritis, and less interest in the happenings of the home may be because he can't see or hear things as he used to, so he is less aware of what's going on around him. See your veterinarian for a checkup, spend additional time with your dog, and include him as much as his energy level and interest dictates. Separation anxiety is a behavior problem common to the older dog, particularly if there have been changes in the home. Older dogs are more set in their ways, and not as adaptable as puppies.

Life Expectancy

Old age comes earlier or later depending on the dog's health and their breed. Small breeds generally live longest, with a life expectancy of 15 years of more. Medium to large breeds generally live for ten to 14 years. Giant breeds age more quickly; their shorter life expectancy of approximately ten years means the signs of old age appear earlier.

Understand Your Older Dog

Most behavioral changes in older dogs are a result of a medical condition. Monitor your dog's health and work with your veterinarian to make your dog's senior years comfortable for him. He has special needs as he ages; when you recognize the signals your older dog sends you'll be better able to respond appropriately.

Older dogs may have trouble dealing with changes to their owners' schedule if it disrupts their routine, and may fear being alone because their deteriorating senses make them feel more vulnerable. The best way to deal with this is to make your departure and returns calm and matter-of-fact, regardless of the anxiety-based behavior your dog exhibits. When you return home, wait until he is calm before acknowledging him at all. You will be tempted to soothe him in an attempt to calm him, but this can communicate to him that his anxiety is valid and therefore prolong his behavior. Try to arrange for some company for your dog at home; a change in his environment could produce further stress and anxiety. Your dog may bark more than he used to, whether you are home or not. Barking when you are away may be a symptom of his separation anxiety, but it is also seen in older dogs who don't experience this. It makes sense: if their sight and hearing are not what they were they can't identify potential threats as easily so may bark to repel what could be a danger—people, other animals, even furniture—instead. Housetraining accidents are also common in older dogs. They are another symptom of separation anxiety and can also be explained due to decreased mobility. If your dog can't move as fast as he used to, he may not be able to prevent himself from soiling inside the house.

Aggression is often seen in older dogs, even if they lived the majority of their life as the most docile of dogs. Barking and growling are defense mechanisms that become especially important if your dog can no longer rely on his sense of hearing or sight. They may also be a sign or injury or pain: your dog is barking to prevent anyone getting too close and touching the sensitive areas, or he growls and snaps when those areas are touched because of the pain it causes. At the first sign of aggression, have your dog checked by your veterinarian to determine if there is a health problem and find out what you can do to make him more comfortable.

Your dog's sleeping patterns may change. He may sleep more often and more heavily or he may be up much of the night, with the latter scenario indicating a possible medical condition that is keeping him up because of pain. The frequent need to urinate that accompanies old age may also be keeping him awake. Senior dogs are also more sensitive to hard surfaces, colder temperatures, and drafts, so make sure he has a soft bed to sleep on and the temperature is comfortable.

 Dog Fact

Older dogs may not like domestic change, but they may enjoy a change in scenery once in awhile. Car rides for mobility-impaired dogs, or short walks and time in the park are generally still welcome.

GLOSSARY

Agility: A judged competitive event. Dogs are trained to manage obstacles such as tunnels, bridges, and high jumps, by following the voice and hand signals of their owner/handler.

Alpha: The highest-ranked or most dominant pack member.

Bark: A short, sharp cry. Duration, tone, and rhythm vary.

Bay: A prolonged bark. Often used by dogs of the hunting breed, such as hounds.

Blowing the Coat: Seasonal coat-shedding to adjust to temperature changes.

Breed: A dog classification based on heritage. For example: Boxer, Cocker Spaniel, Australian Cattle Dog.

Canid: Any of a family of carnivorous animals including dogs, wolves, coyotes, foxes, and jackals.

Canine: An animal of the family Canidae, which includes dogs.

Canine Distemper: Viral infectious disease in dogs.

Coat: The dog's hair covering.

Corded: Type of coat, characterized by long, narrow mats of hair.

Crate: A portable cage made of plastic or metal, used to contain dogs or transport them.

Crossbred: A dog whose parents are from two different breeds.

Dam: The female parent.

Dander: Small skin scales that can cause an allergic reaction in sensitive individuals.

Defensive-aggressive: Fear-based aggressive behavior that is directed at any perceived challenge.

Dominance: Assertive and superiority behavior directed at people and animals.

Dominant: Alpha dog of a pack, or one that displays dominance behavior over other pack members.

Dominant-aggressive: Overconfident and threatening aggressive behavior that is directed at any perceived challenge.

Double Coat: The combination of an undercoat with an outer coat, breed-specific.

Dysplasia: Abnormality of development, especially of the hip or elbow.

Ear Carriage: The way the dog's ears are held: erect, back, flattened. Can indicate mood and intentions combined with other body language cues.

Ear Mange: Condition caused by ear mites, which causes itching and scratching. Ear appearance is red and can be crusty.

Ear Mites: A tiny parasite that is attracted to the ear canal of dogs, and causes intense irritation.

Feral Dog: A dog living in a fully wild state.

Growl: Low-pitched, throaty vocalization.

Hip Dysplasia: A common and debilitating genetic disease of the hips.

Hot Spots: Surface skin infections common to dogs; they generally appear as circular patches and can be painfully itchy.

Kennel: Backyard doghouse, or a commercial establishment used for a group of dogs.

Lead: A length of leather or rope used in dog training and walking, one end held by the owner/handler and the other end attached to the dog's collar.

Leash: A length of leather or rope used in dog training and walking, one end held by the owner/handler and the other end attached to the dog's collar.

Litter: The puppy or puppies of one birth.

Pack Leader: Dominant individual, characterized by authoritative and calm leadership of pack members.

Pedigree: The written record of a dog's genealogy.

Puppy Mill: Place in which puppies are bred, typically in inhumane conditions, for sale to dealers and pet stores.

Purebred: A dog with parents of the same breed.

Scent Marking: Use of urine to mark territory, and communicate with other dogs.

Separation Anxiety: Fear or anxiety-based condition in which dogs exhibit distress and behavior problems when left alone.

Single Coat: Coat that is one layer thick, with no undercoat.

Socialization: The exposure of dogs to new people, animals, and places, to aid in their positive development.

Submissive Urination: Instinctive act of urination to show subordination in the presence of a more dominant or alpha pack member.

Undercoat: A dense second coat that is underneath the topcoat, and is breed specific.

Whine: Nasal cry, varying in pitch and volume.

ACKNOWLEDGMENTS

*F*amily and friends: Maryann, Glenn, Beth, Chrysi, Lindsey, Ben, Joanne, Lorraine—thank you.

PICTURE CREDITS

Page 1	© Isselee | Dreamstime	37 Right	© Toddlaudman | Dreamstime
8	© Ichessell | Dreamstime	38 Left	© Tobkatrina | Dreamstime
10	© Ankevanwyk | Dreamstime	39	© Kamelot | Dreamstime
11 Left	© Fesus | Dreamstime	40	© Andreynl | Dreamstime
11 Right	© Perkus | Dreamstime	41 Left	© Anna63 | Dreamstime
12	© Speedo101 | Dreamstime	41 Right	© Eriklam | Dreamstime
13	© Eriklam | Dreamstime	42	© Toddlaudman | Dreamstime
14 Left	© Isselee | Dreamstime	43	© Henkupenk | Dreamstime
	(and throughout)	44	© Willeecole | Dreamstime
14 Right	© Egophoto | Dreamstime	45	© Eriklam | Dreamstime
15	© Stangot | Dreamstime	46	© Eriklam | Dreamstime
16	© Isselee | Dreamstime	47	© Isselee | Dreamstime
17 Left	© Isselee | Dreamstime	48 Right	© Klaus23 | Dreamstime
17 Center-left	© Chrishowey | Dreamstime	49	© Shhaase | Dreamstime
17 Center-right	© Isselee | Dreamstime	51 Left	© Willeecole | Dreamstime
17 Right	© Gelpi | Dreamstime	52	© Isselee | Dreamstime
18 Left	© Isselee | Dreamstime	53 Left	© Luchschen | Dreamstime
18 Right	© Isselee | Dreamstime	53 Right	© Lauren0788 | Dreamstime
19	© Adogslifephoto | Dreamstime	54 Left	© Isselee | Dreamstime
20	© Pumba1 | Dreamstime	54 Right	© PhotobunnyUK | Dreamstime
21 Left	© Eriklam | Dreamstime	55 Left	© Shevs | Dreamstime
21 Right	© Isselee | Dreamstime	55 Right	© C-foto | Dreamstime
22 Top-right	© Kuzma | Dreamstime	56 Right	© Willeecole | Dreamstime
22 Bottom-right	© Adogslifephoto | Dreamstime	57	© Zrelenenkyyyuriy | Dreamstime
23	© Isselee | Dreamstime	58	© Isselee | Dreamstime
24	© Isselee | Dreamstime	59 Right	© Zudy-box | iStockphoto
25	© Maszas | Dreamstime	60 Right	© Spxchrome | iStockphoto
26	© Kenhurst | Dreamstime	61	© GlobalP | iStockphoto
27	© Gelpi | Dreamstime	62	© Belterz | iStockphoto
29	© Iofoto | Dreamstime	64	© Innocent | Dreamstime
30	© Kourafas5 | Dreamstime	66	© Photowitch | Dreamstime
31	© Jivanchild | Dreamstime	68	© Nejron | Dreamstime
32	© Laures | Dreamstime	69	© Aaleksander | Dreamstime
33	© Willeecole | Dreamstime	70	© Willeecole | Dreamstime
34	© Eriklam | Dreamstime	71	© YuriyGreene | iStockphoto
36 Left	© Chrishowey | Dreamstime	72	© 1905HKN | iStockphoto
36 Right	© Sparkmom | Dreamstime	73 Top	© Zrelenenkyyyuriy | Dreamstime

131	© Sparkmom | Dreamstime		173 Left	© Websubstance | Dreamstime
132	© Ivonnewierink | Dreamstime		173 Right	© TomN | Dreamstime
133	© Goldenkb | Dreamstime		175	© Pieter82 | Dreamstime
135	© Corazonphoto | Dreamstime		176	© Adogslifephoto | Dreamstime
136	© Eastwestimaging | Dreamstime		177 Right	© Isselee | Dreamstime
138	© Anirav | Dreamstime		178 Right	© Momcilog | Dreamstime
139	© Eastwestimaging | Dreamstime		179 Left	© Dmccale | Dreamstime
140 Right	© Nicmac | Dreamstime		179 Right	© Cringuette | Dreamstime
141	© Alphababy | Dreamstime		181	© Isselee | Dreamstime
142	© Iofoto | Dreamstime		182	© YuriArcurs | Dreamstime
143 Top	© Godfer | Dreamstime		184	© Maloy40 | Dreamstime
143 Bottom	© Willecole | Dreamstime		185	© Websubstance | Dreamstime
144	© Eriklam | Dreamstime		187	© Alenkasm | Dreamstime
146 Right	© C-foto | Dreamstime		188	© Cdfoto | Dreamstime
147	© Photowitch | Dreamstime		191	© Peter.Kirillov | Dreamstime
148 Right	© Willeecole | Dreamstime		192	© Andresr | Dreamstime
149	© Cenorman | Dreamstime			
150	© Carebott | Dreamstime			
151	© Goldenkb | Dreamstime			
153	© Willeecole | Dreamstime			
154	© Tobkatrina | Dreamstime			
156	© RyanJLane | iStockphoto			
157 Left	© Ncn18 | Dreamstime			
158	© MarkCoffeePhoto | Dreamstime			
159	© Ivonnwierwink | Dreamstime			
160	© PeterKirillov | Dreamstime			
161	© Justmeyo | Dreamstime			
162 Right	© Flory63 | Dreamstime			
163	© Margojh | Dreamstime			
164	© Rbbrdckybk | Dreamstime			
165 Left	© Achilles | Dreamstime			
165 Right	© Silverfish81 | Dreamstime			
167 Left	© Klaus23 | Dreamstime			
168	© Ioanniss | Dreamstime			
169	© Raywoo | Dreamstime			
170	© Tobkatrina | Dreamstime			
171	© Johan63 | Dreamstime			
172	© Gigi1807 | Dreamstime			

BIBLIOGRAPHY

Aloff, Brenda, *Aggression in Dogs.*
Washington: Dogwise Publishing, 2004.

Coppinger, Raymond, and Lorna Coppinger, *Dogs*.
Chicago: The University of Chicago Press, 2002.

Coren, Stanley, *How to Speak Dog*.
New York: Simon & Schuster, 2001.

Coren, Stanley, *How Dogs Think*.
New York: Free Press, 2004.

Dodman, Nicholas, *Dogs Behaving Badly*.
New York: Bantam Books, 2000.

Donaldson, Jean, *The Culture Clash*.
California: James & Kenneth Publishers, 1996.

Dunbar, Ian, *Dog Behavior*.
New York: Howell Book House, 1999.

Fennell, Jan, *The Dog Listener*.
New York: HarperCollins Inc., 2004.

Fogle, Bruce, *The Dog's Mind*.
New York: Macmillan Publishing Company, 1992.

Geller, Tamar, and Andrea Cagan, *The Loved Dog*.
New York: Simon Spotlight Entertainment, 2007.

Grim, Randy, and Melinda Roth, *Don't Dump the Dog*.
New York: Skyhorse Publishing, 2009.

Horowitz, Alexandra, *Inside of A Dog*.
New York: Scribner, 2009.

Kilcommons, Brian, and Sarah Wilson,
Good Owners, *Great Dogs*.
New York: Warner Books, 1992.

McConnell, Patricia B., *How to Be the Leader of the Pack ... and Have Your Dog Love You for It*.
McConnell Publishing Ltd., 1996.

McConnell, Patricia B., *For the Love of a Dog*.
New York: Ballantine Books, 2007.

Millan, Cesar, and Melissa Jo Peltier,
How to Raise the Perfect Dog.
New York: Harmony Books, 2009.

Millan, Cesar, and Melissa Jo Peltier,
Be the Pack Leader.
New York: Three Rivers Press, 2007.

Miller, Pat, *The Power of Positive Dog Training*.
New Jersey: Wiley Publishing Inc., 2008.

Moore, Arden, *The Dog Behavior Answer Book*.
Massachusetts: Storey Publishing, 2006.

Rugaas, Turid, *On Talking Terms with Dogs: Calming Signals*.
Washington: Dogwise Publishing, 1997 and 2006.

Scott, John Paul, and John L. Fuller, *Genetics and the Social Behavior of the Dog*.
Chicago: The University of Chicago Press Ltd., 1974.

RESOURCES AND FURTHER INFORMATION:

Breed information
http://www.canadasguidetodogs.com/
http://www.dogsincanada.com/
http://www.ckc.ca/en/
http://dogpage.ca/

Adoption and rescue
http://www.adoptananimal.ca/
http://www.projectjessie.ca/
http://www.humanesociety.com/
http://www.wspa.ca/
http://www.animalliberationfront.com/

Training:
http://www.cappdt.ca/public/jpage/1/p/Home/content.do
http://www.dogskool.com/
http://www.aspcabehavior.org/articles/50/Canine-Body-Language.aspx

Project Maddie:
http://www.projectmaddie.blogspot.com/

What do dogs know?
http://www.stanleycoren.com/

INDEX

Adolescent dogs 93, 94, 171, 173, 175

Aggression 12, 33, 49, 50, 51, 54, 57, 58, 59,
    63, 71, 85, 86, 95, 124, 134, 135, 145, 170,
    173, 178-9, 180
    Dealing with 12, 88-90, 93, 94-5

Agility as game 162, 180

Alertness 47, 49, 50, 53

Alpha status 14, 79, 80, 89, 90, 94, 134,
    143, 166, 180

Anthropomorphizing of dog behavior 9, 11,
    101, 137

Anxiety and fear, signs of 50, 68, 70, 93, 96,
    118, 133, 178-9

Appeasement behavior 54, 66

Attention seeking behavior 27, 64, 65, 66, 67,
    69, 72, 110, 116, 144

Attention, requirement for 25, 64, 67, 69, 94,
    148, 157

Ball games 162, 164, 165, 167

Barking and communication 68-73, 180

Baying 63, 180

Begging for food 112-13, 144

Behavioral problems, dealing with 88

Body language, canine 8, 9, 13, 14, 46, 47, 48, 59,
    69, 73, 83, 85, 89, 124, 132, 134, 137, 155, 170

Body language, human 8, 12, 14, 41, 47, 101, 132,
    133, 137

Boredom 97, 98, 102, 103, 108, 116, 121,
   123, 160, 169
Breeds and types 16-17, 23, 24, 25, 180

Canine-canine interaction 31, 39, 53, 59,
   84-7, 110, 136
Canine-human interaction 11, 12, 14, 27, 28,
   48, 59, 69, 73, 95, 101, 132
Cause and effect, dogs and 144, 146
Chewing as a problem 9, 96-7
Children and dogs 21, 33, 63, 103, 133, 136, 145
Clicker training 147
Coats 18, 13, 56, 125, 126, 180
"Come" command 155, 158
Communicating with dogs 13, 138-43
Companionship, need for 25, 64, 70, 77, 96, 97, 121
Compulsive behavior 117

Dance as play 161
Dander and allergies 19, 180
Deaf dogs 155
Deference by dogs 9, 48
Development 40, 97
Digging, by dogs 102-6, 108
Discipline, need for 81, 86
Dog behavior, interpreting 9
Dog crate 31, 98, 180
Dog proofing houses 30, 100
Dog senses 34-45
Dominance, dogs and 50, 94, 110, 132, 134,
   135, 175, 180
Dominance training 146, 148
"Down" command 154, 158
Dysplasia 125, 180

Ears, dogs' 42, 47, 125, 131, 180
Energy levels 21
Excitement, displays of 55, 59, 63, 66, 68,
   68, 115, 159

Exercise 21, 23, 27, 70, 97, 105, 152, 160
Eye contact, significance of 12, 49, 53, 134-5

Fearful behavior 50, 54, 63, 71, 80, 85, 93, 94,
   118, 134, 145, 170, 174, 175
"Find it" game 168
Friendliness, signs of 50

Good behavior 27, 31, 33, 55, 65, 93, 94, 111,
   112, 113, 148, 150
Grass eating and vomiting 120-1
Grooming 129
Growling 58-9, 60-1, 181

Hand signals 35, 36, 155, 158, 159
Health and communication 13, 177, 178
Hearing, canine 39, 40, 41-2
"Heel" command 166
Hide and seek 165
Hierarchy 11, 28, 33, 79, 87, 89, 95, 133, 134, 166
Hoarding instinct 107, 109
Home health check 67, 124-7, 128-30
Housetraining 28, 48, 178
Howling and communication 74-5, 77
Human voice and contact 12, 14, 135

Ill health 65, 67, 124-31

Jumping through hoops 163
Jumping, inappropriate 110-11, 161, 173

King complex 60

Leashes 28, 52, 59, 181
Learned behaviors, inappropriate 110-13, 144
Learning 144-8
Litters, dogs and behavior in 27, 84, 85, 86, 134,
   170, 171, 174, 181

Medical attention, requirements for 115, 117, 124, 128, 131

Mixed breed dogs 24

Mixed messages and dogs 57, 135, 138-41

New dog and new home 26-31, 65, 137

Obedience classes and training 54, 59, 63, 66, 71, 145, 162

Obstacle course game 166

Older dogs 13, 93, 115, 125, 176-9

Overheating 114-15, 166

Pack dynamics 8, 11, 28, 63, 74, 75, 77, 78-83, 89, 90, 148, 156, 175, 175-6, 181

Pain and dogs 13, 49, 63, 93, 130, 177, 179

Panting 50, 114, 115, 127, 129, 166

Play bow 50, 51, 85

Play, canine 50, 51, 55, 60, 73, 85, 86, 105, 160-9

Positive reinforcement 148, 151

Problem behavior, dealing with 80-1, 88-90, 173

Punishment, inappropriateness of 94, 157

Puppies 22, 64, 83, 84, 116, 134, 166, 170-1, 173, 174-5

Purebred dogs 24, 181

Puzzle play 167

Retrieving games 164, 165

Rewarding good behavior 31, 65, 69, 112, 142, 148, 152, 157, 159, 173

Rolling in inappropriate materials 122-3

Search games 167, 168

Selecting a dog 16

Separation anxiety 67, 103, 123, 177, 178, 181

Shedding hair 18, 21, 22, 126

Sign language and dogs 35, 36, 155, 158, 159

Simon says (game) 162

"Sit" command 111, 152, 158

Smell, dog's sense of 37-9, 40

Sociability 21

Social cognition 52

Socialization 42, 59, 90, 92, 93, 123, 145, 148, 170-1, 174, 181

Status in family, establishing dog's 33, 63, 67, 79-80, 89, 111, 135

"Stay" command 111, 150, 153, 158

Storm phobia 12, 14, 118-19

Submission, signs of 9, 47, 48, 49, 50, 51, 54, 56, 57, 134, 137, 170, 181

Submissive role, encouraging 33, 80

Tail chasing 116-17

Tails and body language 53

Taste, dog's sense of 40, 42, 44

Teething 97, 101, 127

Temperature control 103

Touch, dog's sense of 40, 42

Toys 28, 31, 55, 65, 66, 97, 98, 100, 105, 106, 107, 111, 112, 140, 148, 164, 168, 169, 173

Training 27, 60, 67, 70, 80, 89, 93, 97, 103, 105, 145-59, 162, 171, 173, 174, 177

Urinating 9, 48, 179, 181

Vision, canine 35-6, 39, 40

Vomiting 121, 127

Whining 64-7, 181

Whiskers (vibrissae) 42, 45

Wolf ancestry, impact of 75, 77, 78, 107, 111, 121, 123